101 Perfect Chocolate Chip Cookies

Gwen Steege

STOREY BOOKS

Schoolhouse Road
Pownal, Vermont 05261

The mission of Storey Communications is to serve our customers
by publishing practical information that encourages personal independence
in harmony with the environment.

■ ■ ■ ■

Edited by Jeanée Ledoux
Cover design by Meredith Maker
Front cover photograph © Steven Mark Needham/Envision; back cover
  photographs by Giles Prett
Interior photographs by Giles Prett
Text design by Betty Kodela and Susan Bernier
Text production by Susan Bernier, Leslie Constantino, and Jennifer Jepson Smith
Illustrations by Alison Kolesar
Indexed by Peggy Holloway

Printed in the United States by Von Hoffmann Graphics
10 9 8 7 6 5 4 3 2 1

Library of Congress Cataloging-in-Publication Data

Steege, Gwen, 1940–
    101 perfect chocolate chip cookie / Gwen Steege
      p. cm.
    ISBN 1-58017-312-8 (pbk.)
  TX772. 575 2000
  641.8'654—dc21

00-055608

CONTENTS

THE SEARCH FOR
THE PERFECT
CHOCOLATE
CHIP COOKIE

"If it's not chocolate, it's not dessert!" That's been our family motto for years, no matter how small, or how special, the occasion. And we're surely not alone in our passion. Since its discovery centuries ago, the very word *chocolate* has always conjured up images and aromas of rich sauces, elegant mousses, steaming hot drinks, delectable fudges, and moist, dark cakes.

This superstar ingredient appears in dozens of favorite desserts and drinks, but one of the most universally popular is that particularly American invention, chocolate chip cookies. Warm from the oven, they're the perfect offering to a cranky child, the supreme appeasement for a lover's quarrel, the ideal gift to a special friend, and the ultimate bedtime snack.

In 1987, it was the bedtime snack that struck the fancy of Chester Soling, then owner of The Orchards, an inn in the Berkshires of western Massachusetts. The Orchards offered their guests fresh-baked chocolate chip cookies and cold milk by their beds every night. And these weren't just any chocolate chip cookies. They were baked from recipes submitted to a nationwide contest sponsored by the inn. The search for the perfect chocolate chip cookie led to this book, which includes the winners and a selection of more than 100 of the 2,600 entries received from almost every state, as well as from Italy, Canada, and Mexico.

The contributors to this book — the contestants — describe how their recipes are special or how they came to them. Some share family recipes brought to North America from Europe over a century ago. Others relate how their experiences influence the way they think about food: An anthropologist teaches her children to consider where ingredients are grown and how they became locally available; a wheat

Pure Heaven

If you describe your favorite chocolate dessert as "divine," you aren't the first to connect chocolate to the heavens. In fact, the evergreen trees on which the cocoa bean grows come from the scientific genus *Theobroma,* which translates from the Latin as "food for the gods."

farmer's daughter from Saskatchewan, Canada, remembers the magic that unrefined flour put into any recipe; a parent describes the enjoyment a batch of cookies brought to residents in a Ronald McDonald House, a facility for critically ill children and their families.

Another important contributor to this book is Orchards pastry chef Heather Andrus, whose patient advice and guidance helped educate me about the many refinements of chocolate chip cookie baking. Two of Heather's own favorite cookie recipes appear on pages 29 and 30.

Because each chocolate chip cookie recipe included in this collection has particular significance and appeal, it wasn't easy to choose a winner! As you bake your way through this book, you may find your own special favorite recipe, or, better still, you can take off from these tips, ideas, and recipes to create your own perfect chocolate chip cookie.

A Word about Chocolate

Europeans first learned about chocolate in 1502 when Columbus brought cocoa beans back to Spain from his fourth and last exploration of the New World. A few years later, the Spanish conquistador Cortez observed the Aztec emperor Montezuma and his household enjoying golden goblets full of a cold drink concocted of unsweetened chocolate, vanilla, and ground hot peppers. The Aztecs called this brew *xoco-latl*, meaning bitter water. Legend has it that Montezuma alone consumed 50 cups of this brew a day, while his large household downed another 2,000 cups. Small wonder it was so popular, for the Aztecs believed xoco-latl bestowed energy.

Freezer Treats

- Sandwich your favorite ice cream between two giant-sized cookies, wrap in foil, and freeze.

- Make chocolate chip cookie ice cream by crumbling leftover cookies and adding them to homemade vanilla or chocolate ice cream.

Who Needs Tea?

Chocolate was first manufactured in the western hemisphere in Dorchester, Massachusetts, in 1765 — relatively late considering its popularity in Europe. Only a few years after that, however, it became an important substitute for tea when colonists sought to avoid the British tea tax. Thomas Jefferson praised it as superior to both tea and coffee for health and nourishment.

The Spanish improved the bitter chocolate drink by adding some sugar and a stick of cinnamon along with the vanilla. This culinary discovery was so special that the recipe for processing cocoa beans was a guarded secret in monasteries for nearly 100 years. An Italian traveler let loose the secret when he smuggled some chocolate to the Italian courts, and by the mid-1550s, there were large chocolate factories in many southern European cities. From there the magic spread to Austria, France, and England, where in the mid-17th century chocolate houses, like coffee houses, became favorite meeting places of the wealthy cognoscente. In France, King Louis XIV even established a position of Royal Chocolate Maker to the King. Later, Napoleon took chocolate along on his military campaigns for its quick energy value.

Chocolate was rich material for 19th-century inventiveness. About mid-century, the British devised a method for making a bar of solid chocolate. About 25 years later, the Swiss found a way to incorporate condensed milk into chocolate, thus producing milk chocolate. These innovations, coupled with the century's growing love affair with technology and machinery, made the large-scale production of chocolate possible and opened a realm of possibilities for the use and distribution of chocolate that could satisfy even the most ardent chocolate lovers.

The Birth of Chocolate Chip Cookies

It seems a long way from Montezuma's heady, bitter chocolate drink to American chocolate chip cookies. The story begins at another New England inn, one in eastern Massachusetts, more than 70 years ago. In 1930, Ken and Ruth Wakefield opened a restaurant in a colonial house in Whitman, Massachusetts, on the heavily traveled road between Boston and the old whaling town of New Bedford. Known as the Toll House Inn from the early days when stagecoaches stopped there to pay a toll at the gates, the restaurant was highly regarded for its excellent food and hospitable service. But real fame came to the inn with Ruth Wakefield's impulsive invention of a brand-new kind of cookie.

Like many serendipitous discoveries, this one was really an accident. One of Mrs. Wakefield's favorite recipes was a colonial butter cookie called "Butter Drop-Do's." When she one day ran out of nuts while making them, she grabbed a Nestlé semisweet chocolate bar, broke it into bits, and mixed it into the dough, expecting the chocolate to melt into the cookies as they baked. But the result was far better than she dreamed — delightfully gooey little chunks of chocolate perfectly complemented the buttery, crunchy cookie. Her new "Chocolate Crispies," as she called them, quickly became favorites with customers.

Add Some Nestlé Inventiveness

Soon after Ruth Wakefield's recipe was published in a Boston newspaper, sales of Nestlé's semisweet chocolate bar skyrocketed in the Boston area, causing Nestlé officials to investigate the source of the success. When they learned about the new cookie, they thought, if New Englanders loved this cookie so much, why not make it easy for everyone to use Nestlé bars in this recipe? Nestlé decided to manufacture their bars scored so that they would break readily. They eventually marketed a special chopper for cutting the chocolate up into the proper-sized pieces, and in 1939, the Nestlé company began making chocolate bits in that now-so-familiar morsel form. In the 1940s, they bought the Toll House name from the Wakefields and ever since have printed the original recipe on the back of the package. (See page 6 for recipe.)

Original Nestlé Toll House Chocolate Chip Cookies

Reprinted with permission from Nestlé.

2¼ cups flour

1 teaspoon baking soda

1 teaspoon salt

1 cup butter, softened

¾ cup granulated sugar

¾ cup brown sugar, firmly packed

1 teaspoon vanilla extract

2 eggs

12 ounces (2 cups) Nestlé Toll House semisweet chocolate morsels

1 cup chopped nuts

1. In a small bowl, combine the flour, baking soda, and salt; set aside.

2. In a large bowl, combine the butter, granulated sugar, brown sugar, and vanilla extract; beat until creamy. Beat in the eggs. Gradually add the flour mixture. Finally, stir in the Nestlé Toll House semisweet chocolate morsels and nuts.

3. Drop by level measuring tablespoonfuls onto ungreased cookie sheets. Bake at 375°F for 9 to 11 minutes.

Yield: 5 dozen

You Get What You Put into It

Before breaking out the pans and diving into the chips, take a minute to learn a bit about the standard ingredients and how to use them. The rules to success are simple: Use the freshest, highest quality ingredients you can find, and treat them properly from the time you bring them home from the store, right through the whole baking process.

First, a bit of honesty: When you look closely at almost any chocolate chip cookie recipe, you'll find that at its core are the simple ingredients in Ruth Wakefield's famous Toll House Cookie. In addition to chocolate chips, you'll find butter, sugar, one or more eggs, flour, leavening, a little flavoring, and maybe some nuts. But change the proportions and even the mixing and baking techniques here and there, add your own secret ingredients, and you get a significantly different cookie, a wholly new variation on the old theme.

The very best way to begin your own search for the perfect chocolate chip cookie is to understand what role each ingredient plays in the basic cookie dough and how to handle it properly. Then, try out the recipes in your own kitchen.

First, of course, you have to get to know the most important ingredient — the chocolate.

Chocolate: From the Tree to Your Kitchen

Although Columbus brought chocolate to Europe at the beginning of the 16th century, the process for producing something wonderful from those unpromising little seeds of the cacao tree was kept secret for many years. In fact, the technology of chocolate making is still considered very complex. Grown only in tropical climates, mostly in West Africa and Central and

Running the Numbers

The United States is now the world's leading producer of chocolate. However, Americans rank only seventh as world consumers of chocolate, eating a meager 10 pounds of chocolate each year — the average Swiss consumes 22 pounds, and in the United Kingdom, each citizen eats 15.4 pounds. It may be best not to contemplate how many pounds we put on if we consume those 10 (plus or minus) pounds of chocolate per year!

Some Chocolaty Vocabulary

Cocoa powder. American-processed chocolate, the product remaining after most of the cocoa butter is removed. This is lower in fat than any other kind of chocolate (about 10 percent cocoa butter remains). If stored airtight, it will stay fresh and high quality almost indefinitely, even without refrigeration. *Breakfast cocoa* has a higher fat content (at least 22 percent). *Dutch-processed cocoa* is treated with a very small amount of alkali, which neutralizes the acids in the liquor and makes the chocolate darker and less bitter than American-processed cocoa; the Dutch cocoa also blends more readily with liquids. If you substitute flourlike cocoa for baking chocolate in recipes, the cookies may turn out cakier.

Instant cocoa contains sugar and dry milk solids for convenience in mixing chocolate-flavored drinks. It should not be substituted for other kinds of chocolate in baking.

Bitter or baking chocolate is produced when pure chocolate liquor, with most of the cocoa butter removed, is cooled and molded into blocks, one square or block equaling 1 ounce.

Semisweet chocolate, the chocolate most commonly packaged as chips, contains at least 35 percent pure chocolate liquor, plus some cocoa butter added back in along with sugar and vanilla.

Bittersweet chocolate is 50 percent pure chocolate liquor, with less sugar than semisweet chocolate.

Sweet dark chocolate is only 15 percent pure liquor; it also contains more sugar.

Milk chocolate contains at least 10 percent chocolate liquor and about 16 percent milk, cream, or dry milk solids, as well as cocoa butter, sugar, and flavorings.

White, or confectioners', chocolate contains no chocolate liquor. By law, it's not chocolate at all. It's made by cooking down milk and sugar until almost solid and then adding cocoa butter and vanilla.

Artificial chocolate may actually contain no chocolate at all. Often some or all of the cocoa butter is replaced by ingredients that give the chocolate a waxy texture.

Chocolate-flavored products do not have enough pure chocolate to meet government standards for real chocolate and may contain vegetable oils and other additives. Premelted liquid chocolate packaged for baking convenience and chocolate syrups fall into this category.

South America, the cacao tree must be eight years old before it produces a fruit, or pod, about the size and shape of a summer squash. Each tree produces 20 to 40 pods, each filled with 25 to 50 one-inch, almond-shaped, creamy violet seeds, or beans. These beans are sun-dried, fermented, cleaned, and blended. Like coffee- or winemakers, each chocolate manufacturer has a special formula for a blend of beans from different countries and different varieties of cacao trees. Once blended, beans are roasted to bring out their flavor and aroma, then hulled.

The process of crushing the beans between stones or steel blades causes them to generate heat and liquefy, which allows the cocoa butter, or cocoa fat, to be extracted under pressure. Cocoa butter is what allows chocolate to melt; it also gives chocolate its special creamy texture. The thick, dark paste that remains after most of the cocoa butter is removed is called *chocolate liquor*. The beans usually yield about equal amounts of cocoa butter and chocolate liquor. From this point you can make any of the various kinds of chocolate called for in cooking and baking, depending upon the percentage of pure chocolate liquor in relation to the other ingredients, such as reintroduced cocoa butter, as well as sugar and milk.

Sweetened chocolate undergoes two additional steps: *refining*, which reduces it to a paste, and *conching*, which assures the smoothness of the finished product — the longer the conching period, the smoother, and also the more expensive, the chocolate. An aging period of up to six months further improves flavor.

Storing Chocolate

Chocolate has a long shelf life: Milk chocolate is good for about six months, and dark chocolate lasts for well over a year

Cocoa as a Substitute

You can substitute cocoa for other kinds of chocolate using the following proportions:

- 3 tablespoons cocoa plus 1 tablespoon butter, margarine, or shortening = 1 square of baking chocolate

- 6 tablespoons cocoa, 7 tablespoons sugar, and ¼ cup butter, margarine, or shortening = 6 ounces (1 cup) of semisweet chocolate chips

- 3 tablespoons cocoa, 4½ tablespoons sugar, and 2⅔ tablespoons butter, margarine, or shortening = 4 ounces of sweet baking chocolate

in a cool (about 60–75°F), dry place. At temperatures above 78°F, the chocolate will begin to melt and the cocoa butter will begin to separate out. In addition, moisture can cause the sugar to melt and condense on the surface of milk or semisweet chocolate. When either of these things happens, a grayish white film may develop on the outside of the chocolate. Although not great-looking, this film, called *bloom*, is harmless and doesn't affect the taste or quality of chocolate used in baking.

You can also freeze chocolate of all kinds for about a year. Chocolate that's been frozen is perfectly acceptable for use in baking, but if you're planning to use the chocolate for anything more complicated, such as candy making, it's best not to freeze it. To avoid having your frozen or refrigerated chocolate "sweat," bring it to room temperature before using it in baking.

Cocoa keeps its freshness and quality almost indefinitely without refrigeration, but it, like all other chocolates, should be kept tightly wrapped so that it won't absorb odors and moisture.

Melting Chocolate

Chocolate must be treated with great respect during melting, for, like an eccentric relative, it has some funny ways if not handled properly. For quick, even melting, break or chop the chocolate into small pieces with a chef's knife or grind it in a blender or food processor, then place it over heat. The safest way to melt all kinds of chocolate is to put it in the top of a double boiler over hot, but not boiling, water. This way you won't have to worry about scorching it or getting steam into it. If you attempt to melt it over direct heat, be sure to use very low heat and a heavy saucepan and stir it constantly. Melt very small amounts in a heatproof cup placed in a pan of hot water.

Reheating Chocolate

If melted chocolate cools too much and hardens before you have a chance to incorporate it into your dough, you can reheat it using the same precautions as for first-time melting. Always be careful not to let chocolate get too hot; it burns very easily.

Microwaving is a convenient way to melt chocolate if you're careful and patient. Unwrap and chop blocks of chocolate and place them in a microwaveable cup or bowl. With your microwave set on high (600 watts), microwave for 1 minute, checking after 30 seconds. Stir it with a rubber spatula to encourage even melting, then microwave for another minute, checking again after 30 seconds. Allow the chocolate to stand and complete melting for several minutes, then stir it again. You may need to return the chocolate to the microwave for an additional 30 seconds if some lumps still remain. The length of time necessary varies with the amount of chocolate you need to melt. The trick is not to microwave too long, or the chocolate will harden and burn.

So Many Choices

It's fun to experiment with all the various-sized chocolates on the market, from minichips, which ensure that tiny bits of chocolate will be well dispersed throughout the cookie, through maxichips and chocolate chunks and right up to pieces of candy, such as Hershey's Kisses or M&Ms. Imagine what kind of texture you want when you bite into your cookie: Minichips may melt and get lost in the dough while the cookies bake, but maxichips may be just too much chocolate for your idea of the perfect cookie. If none of what's on the grocery shelf seems just right, you have the whole world of chocolate bars to play around with.

Have a chocolate-tasting session — that shouldn't be onerous! Buy several different brands, including your supermarket's generic brand, and also sample different kinds of chocolate: bittersweet, semisweet, milk, and sweet. Number them and keep a list separately so that you won't know the

Seize the Day — but Not the Chocolate!

Too-high temperatures or moisture from steam or wet utensils may cause the chocolate to become stiff, grainy, and unworkable. This dismaying event is called *seizing*. You can sometimes save the day by vigorously beating in 1 teaspoon solid vegetable shortening for every 2 ounces of chocolate. (Do not use butter. Because it contains water, it may worsen the problem.)

You can avoid seizing if you melt a couple of tablespoons of another ingredient from the recipe, such as butter, along with the chocolate.

Many people feel that good chocolate, like fine wine, improves over a period of many years.

kind or brand you're sampling and be swayed by preconceived notions of what's best. Smell each sample, taste it, let it melt in your mouth, and then drink some water and wait before moving on to the next so that you can really savor each one individually. Judge the relative smoothness or graininess, sweetness or bitterness, waxiness or creaminess of each chocolate. Every manufacturer's recipe for processing and mixing chocolate is different, and their products are therefore distinctly different as well. Make a list in order of your preference. This blind approach may offer some surprises, and it certainly will be fun. The most expensive imported chocolate may not, after all, be the one you choose over more readily available, less expensive kinds.

If you can't make up your mind, try combinations of two or more chocolates, such as white, milk, and semisweet. You'll find that the variety adds texture as well as flavor to the cookies. When you make chocolate chip cookies, look for recipes in this book that use your favorite types, or substitute what you like best for what's called for in the recipe — the first step in inventing your own special recipe.

Once the hard decision of what kind of chocolate to use is out of the way, you're ready to deal with the basic cookie dough. Now we get to tenderness, and that's determined by the next two important ingredients: butter and sugar.

Butter, Margarine, or Shortening: An Awesome Triplet

Excellent cookie recipes call for butter, margarine, shortening, or even vegetable oil. Each of these fats produces a significantly different flavor and texture, which means that each has strong advocates. Some recipes call for more than one in an attempt to get the best of several worlds. The temperature of these ingredients affects the result, too. You'll find that many recipes indicate that the butter or margarine should be room temperature before using, while some require chilled or even frozen butter and others call for melting the butter first.

Some recipes in this book use butter and margarine in equal parts or leave the choice of which to use up to you. But if a recipe calls for just butter, the results really count on the special flavor and texture that only butter contributes. If you substitute another fat for the butter, your cookies will be slightly, or in some cases substantially, different. In any case, don't use whipped margarine, which has added water that can really upset the end result.

Many recipes in this book call for unsalted, or sweet, butter. In the days before adequate refrigeration, salt was used as a preservative in butter. Nowadays, because different brands vary in saltiness, many cooks prefer using unsalted butter to regulate the salt better in their baking. And many cooks simply prefer the smooth taste of unsalted butter.

Pure, solid, all-vegetable shortening is also quite good in cookie baking. Vegetable shortening is the result of hydrogenating, or adding hydrogen, to vegetable oils, such as polyunsaturated soybean, palm, and sunflower oils. Rather than breaking with a snap, a cookie made with shortening is a "short" cookie — one that breaks solidly and thickly, like a peanut butter cookie or shortbread. You may like a combination of shortening and butter. If you substitute shortening for some or all of the butter or margarine in a recipe, cut the amount by about one-fifth.

THE SALT OF THE EARTH

If you substitute salted for sweet butter, you might want to reduce the amount of salt called for in the recipe.

Cookies need sugar not only to sweeten the dough but to make it more tender. In this book when the word "sugar" alone is listed, use white, granulated sugar. Many chocolate chip cookie recipes call for brown sugar — light or dark — as well as granulated sugar. Dark brown sugar gets its color and stronger flavor from the molasses that's added to it. The term "brown sugar" alone in recipes usually refers to light brown sugar, but you can always use dark brown sugar if you prefer its flavor.

Some cooks think corn syrup makes a chewy cookie with a crisp outside. If this trait is a must-have, try some of the recipes that use corn syrup (see index).

You can also use honey as a sweetener, substituting it for all or part of the sugar called for in the recipe. Use about three-quarters as much honey as you would have used sugar — for example, if the recipe calls for 1 cup sugar, use ¾ cup honey. Cut back on the amount of liquid in the recipe. Cookies with honey will be moister and softer than those made with sugar.

Soften Up

Brown sugar will harden to stone if not stored in a tightly closed container. A piece of bread placed in the sugar can help keep the sugar soft. Just don't use seasoned bread; it will "share" its flavor with the sugar.

You can soften brown sugar by placing it in a shallow pan, misting it with a little water, and putting it in a 300°F oven for 15 minutes or so until it has improved. Or, place the sugar in a shallow dish and put both the sugar and a small bowl or cup of water in a microwave oven for about 3 minutes on high. If the sugar has not improved, continue microwaving for 1 minute at a time, checking the progress after each minute.

Eggs: Try a Little Tenderness

Eggs should always be as fresh as possible. They contribute to the moistness, lightness, and tenderness of a cookie. When you cream the butter and sugar and then beat in the eggs, you're incorporating air into your cookie batter, ensuring light, tender cookies. The fresher the eggs, the more air can be beaten in. You'll find that you can beat room temperature eggs to a greater volume. Most of the following cookie recipes do not require that you beat the eggs before adding them to the butter and sugar.

Unless otherwise noted, use large, Grade A eggs. Brown and white are equally fine. Just keep thinking, "fresh!"

Vanilla Extract: An Exotic Addition

It's much nicer to use real vanilla extract rather than imitation vanilla flavor in baking. If you're going to the trouble of having all your other ingredients fresh and wonderful, why spoil the whole thing with imitation flavor?

Homemade vanilla extract. It's quite simple as well as less expensive to make your own vanilla extract. Split three or four vanilla beans lengthwise, cut them into 3-inch pieces, and place them in a pint of light rum, tightly corked, for at least a month before using. The longer you can wait, the better the flavor — and aroma!

Flours and Other Grains

In the following recipes, when the word "flour" alone is listed, use all-purpose, unbleached wheat flour — all-purpose, because its mixture of hard, high-gluten, and soft wheats is best

Flavor from Flowers

Vanilla was first brought to Europe from the court of Montezuma by Cortez. The cured fruit of a tropical orchid, most vanilla used in the United States today comes from the island of Madagascar.

Unless specifically
noted otherwise, sift
flour before measuring
it. This is important,
not to rid it of lumps,
but because stored
flour settles, and sifting
"unsettles" it. You may
wish to sift even whole-
wheat flour, then add
back in particles that
do not go through
the sifter.

To measure flour,
spoon it lightly into a
dry-measuring cup.
Level off the excess
with a knife, being
careful not to pack or
shake down the flour
in the process. Finally,
add the other dry
ingredients, such as
baking powder or
baking soda, salt, and
spices, to the sifted
flour, and sift again to
blend everything well.

suited to cookie baking, and unbleached, because it's higher in nutritional value. (After all, if you're indulging in cookies, you might as well make them healthy!) All-purpose flour has had both the outermost part of the grain seed, the *bran*, and the innermost germ removed during the milling process. The flour is then enriched by reintroducing some of the vitamins and minerals lost with the bran and germ. The result is a smooth, white flour that both stores better and produces lighter baked goods than whole wheat flour.

The moisture content of different brands of flour varies somewhat, affecting the amount of liquid required in a recipe. You may need to add a bit more or less flour to a dough to compensate for differences in absorption or the relative humidity in your kitchen. Knowing whether and how much to change a recipe comes with experience and experimentation.

Cake flour. Some cookie recipes call for cake flour, which is made of soft wheats with less gluten. Cake flour produces cookies with a more crumbly texture than those made with all-purpose flour. If you'd like to substitute all-purpose flour for cake flour, use 2 tablespoons less per cup. Be aware that the results still may not be quite the same as if you had used cake flour.

Bread flour is made from hard flours with a higher proportion of gluten. The resulting dough is apt to be elastic and to produce a rather tough cookie. Don't be afraid to experiment: You may like the different effects of various kinds of flours.

Other grains. You can give cookies an extra boost of flavor, texture, and nutrition by incorporating whole-wheat flour, wheat germ, bran, or oatmeal into your dough along with all-purpose flour. Smuggle a secret infusion of good nutrition into snacks by using a bit of soy flour (high in iron, calcium, and protein), bran (fiber), or wheat germ (nutty flavor, combined with good protein and mineral content) in your family's cookies. You don't need to add much of any of these to significantly increase the cookies' nutritional value. The recipes on pages 88–108 are good examples of how well these ingredients work.

Rolled oats are a favorite cookie ingredient. You'll find both regular and quick-cooking oats on the grocery shelves. Which to use is your preference, but don't use instant oatmeal; it's been processed and added to, so it's deprived of the nutty flavor and texture of natural rolled oats. *Quick-cooking oats* have thinner flakes and blend more completely into the cookie dough, while *regular oats* retain their shape and chewiness. Cookies made with regular oats will be crunchier and more crumbly, like granola bars. Some recipes call for *oat flour*, which you can make by whirling oats in the blender or food processor until they are reduced to a fine powder. Part oat flour in a recipe will yield denser, thicker cookies.

Cornstarch. It's even possible to use part cornstarch in place of some of the flour in cookie recipes. This produces a wonderfully crisp cookie.

Leavening: Lighten Up, Please

Baking powder and baking soda are the leaveners in cookies. Without them, we'd end up with hard, unappealing rocks instead of tender, crumbly pastries. In addition to the process of creaming the butter, sugar, and eggs, leavening is another way of incorporating air and lightening the dough.

Both baking powder and baking soda contain an alkaline and an acid that react with each other when moistened to form carbon dioxide gas. The gas makes tiny bubbles that expand in the dough under the heat of baking and leave little air pockets all through the cookies after they cool. The result is crumbly, light cakes and cookies.

WHAT A NUT!

For extra nuttiness and crunch, try lightly toasting rolled oats before using them in baking. To toast oats, spread them in a large baking pan and bake them in a 325°F oven for about 15 minutes, watching and stirring them frequently to avoid burning them.

GOING NUTS

You can chop nuts more easily when they're warm and moist. Both shelled and unshelled nuts keep best (up to a year) frozen.

Double-acting baking powder. Most commonly used in cookie baking, this is a combination of cream of tartar, bicarbonate of soda, and salt. It's referred to as double-acting because it begins its work even in the cold dough, though most of its action takes place while the cookies are baking.

Baking soda. Some recipes call for a small amount of baking soda in addition to the baking powder. Baking soda tends to produce an even more tender cookie. It works only in the presence of an additional acid, such as sour cream, buttermilk, or molasses. When you use baking soda alone as leavening, get the cookies into the oven as quickly as possible. Since it is single-action only and begins to work as soon as moisture hits it, it may lose its power before the heat can set the air pockets and the result will be hard, flat cookies.

Nuts: A Question of Taste

Now we get to serious cookie controversy: Nuts have both staunch advocates and fierce opponents when it comes to chocolate chip cookies. In fact, two-thirds of Americans surveyed recently said "no thanks" to nuts. Still, their flavor, texture, and nutrition tempt many cookie bakers to use them. One Orchards contestant suggested grinding walnuts or almonds rather finely to get a nutty flavor without adding the "lump" that offends those anti-nut folks among us. The real nut lovers prefer not even to chop the nuts, but to simply break up the pieces rather coarsely with their fingers.

You can enhance the flavor of some nuts, such as hazelnuts, by lightly toasting them before use in baking. Spread the nuts thinly and evenly on a large baking sheet and place them in a low oven (300 to 325°F) for about 15 to 20 minutes. Stir them frequently and watch them carefully to avoid burning.

These basic ingredients are only the beginning. If you really want to gild the lily, you're limited only by your taste and imagination. When you get into the recipes, you'll find some with extra chocolate, pinto beans and zucchini, coconut and all kinds of nuts, oranges and apricots, Irish Mist, crème de menthe and other liqueurs, and much more. Look for your favorites and then let yourself be inspired to inventiveness.

Getting Them All Mixed Up

Like the ingredients themselves, the mixing method for chocolate chip cookies doesn't change radically from one recipe to the next. When you do see a difference, be sure to follow the recipe instructions, because they may make a difference in the final result. Generally speaking, however, here's how to proceed.

Once Upon a Pan

You'd think that preparing a baking sheet for cooking would be noncontroversial, but, in fact, every cook has a different idea. Some grease their pans; some don't. Maybe you think you should line your pans instead of greasing them — or even in addition to greasing them. Okay, but should you use aluminum foil or baking parchment? And what kinds of pans, anyway? The Orchards chef recommends using baking parchment because she feels that greasing pans may cause the cookies to spread too much while baking. More cakelike cookies, however, may need pans that are lightly greased to avoid real sticking problems.

And then there's the choice of baking sheet itself. The kind of pan you use can affect a cookie's texture. Since shiny

BETTER
THAN BUTTER

■ ■ ■

If you grease your pans, use margarine, not butter, and be sure to regrease if you cook more than one batch.

Take the Chill Off

Many ingredients need to be brought to room temperature before use: the butter or margarine, to make it soft enough to work with and cream well; the eggs, to make the most of their potential volume; and the chocolate, to prevent it from cooling the batter while baking, thus causing uneven baking.

pans deflect heat and dark ones retain it, cookies may brown too rapidly and burn more easily on dark pans. Thin metal pans can also cause burning because they allow the cookies to bake from underneath. Insulated baking sheets produce a softer cookie.

I like to use heavy, shiny pans with only one raised edge. I line them with parchment paper and usually don't grease them. If you follow this method, you can allow the cookies to set for a minute or two after you take them out of the oven. Then, you can carefully slide both the paper and cookies right off the pan onto trays or racks without disturbing and breaking the warm cookies. Lay down a fresh piece of parchment, and the pans are ready for the next batch.

The kind of baking sheets you use and how you treat them really are up to you and your own experience. Whatever you choose, be sure they'll fit in your oven with 3 or 4 inches to spare all around to ensure proper heat circulation.

Step 1: Getting Started

Make a habit of getting out everything your recipe calls for and organizing it on the counter before you begin to mix things up. This way, you find out before you're halfway into the project that you're flat out of baking powder or that you forgot to buy walnuts. Put everything you will use in one place on the counter, and then move things one by one to another area as you finish with them. This is a great system for the absent-minded, for cooks who are working with children, or for people who are likely to be interrupted: You know that everything in one spot has already been used and that everything else still needs to be added. No more double salting — or forgetting the salt altogether!

Step 2: Preheating the Oven

Since your oven needs about 10 or 15 minutes to preheat, turn it to the proper temperature and arrange the oven racks just before you start to mix up the ingredients. (If you're planning to chill the dough before baking it, wait until shortly before you're ready to bake to preheat the oven. See Step 7.)

Although it's usually easy to mix up a batch of cookies, it's also all too easy to burn them, especially if they contain butter. They're less likely to burn if you place them in the middle or upper part of the oven, so it's best to use only the center rack. If you're too impatient to bake only one tray at a time, put one rack one-third of the way up and the other at two-thirds, then switch the trays from rack to rack about halfway through the baking period. From hard experience, I know that burning happens quickly and irremediably, especially if your oven overheats.

Step 3: Sifting the Dry Ingredients

I like to get the sifting and measuring of dry ingredients out of the way at the start. Usually I sift the flour before measuring and then resift it with other dry ingredients, such as baking powder and salt, before I do anything else. If you sift onto pieces of waxed paper, you'll have fewer bowls to worry about at clean-up. Set the dry ingredients aside until they're needed.

Step 4: Creaming the Butter, Sugar, and Eggs

Creaming means beating the butter until you incorporate so much air that it becomes light and fluffy. While butter should be somewhat softened for this procedure, don't allow it to get too warm or it won't absorb the proper amount of air. As

TIME FOR A TEST

Take a tip from the professionals: From time to time, test your oven temperature with a thermometer to be sure the oven isn't over- (or under-) heating.

the butter changes its texture, gradually add the sugar and continue to cream them thoroughly together. A bit of experience will help you judge when to stop: You want a light, fluffy mixture, but you mustn't let the butter get too soft or it will lose its airiness and get runny, and the cookies will tend to spread.

Most recipes call for adding the eggs one at a time at this point. You don't need to beat them before adding them to the creamed mixture, though it's a good idea to break them into a separate bowl first to avoid getting bits of shell in the batter. As you beat in the eggs, you're continuing to incorporate air into your batter. The more air, the lighter and tenderer the cookies. When the mixture is creamed just right, you'll usually want to stir in the vanilla extract or other flavoring.

Step 5: Combining the Dry with the Moist

Now go back to the dry ingredients you measured and prepared. Add a cup or so of the dry mixture to the creamed, continuing to beat with a wooden spoon. Then add the remaining dry ingredients. At this point, you can get right in and mix the batter with your hands (clean hands, of course, with jewelry removed). Children usually love this technique, and it's easier for them to control all that obstinate dough with their hands than with a spoon, which tends to send globules of batter off in all directions. Blend the dry ingredients completely, until no flour shows — but no longer, or your cookies will be tough.

Step 6: Adding the Goodies

This is the part I like best: stirring in the chocolate chips, nuts, and any other special ingredients. Make sure the chips aren't cold; cold chips chill the dough and cause uneven

One Tough Cookie

One of the most common mistakes that cookie bakers make is overmixing. Result: tough cookies. Pastry Chef Andrus recommends using a wooden spoon to cream the butter and sugar and to beat in the eggs. Then when it's time to mix in all other ingredients, from flour right to chocolate chips, use your hands. You're much less apt to overmix when you use this method.

baking. But they shouldn't be too soft either, or the chocolate will begin to mix in with the batter. Never mix the chips in with an electric mixer. It's likely to chop them up while it spins away, and you'll lose the chips in the batter.

Step 7: Chill Out

Many people like to refrigerate the dough at this point. Chilling the dough seems to blend the flavors together; it also tends to produce a more shapely cookie, one that won't spread all over the pan while baking. And as with pie dough, I've found that chilled dough results in a flakier product.

Step 8: Forming the Cookies

Traditionally, chocolate chip cookies fall into the "drop cookie" category, and most recipes instruct you to drop cookies by teaspoonfuls or tablespoonfuls onto the prepared baking sheets. The easiest way to do this is to use one spoon for scooping up the dough and a second spoon for scraping it off onto the pan. If you like large cookies, use an ice cream scoop with a built-in scraper; a 1½-inch scoop will make a 2½-inch cookie. Or, for a giant 6-inch cookie, use your ⅓-cup dry-measure. Be sure to flatten large cookies somewhat before baking or the centers will never cook through.

An alternative method, even if the recipe doesn't direct it, is to form the dough into balls of whatever size you desire. This is most easily done with chilled dough. You may wish to flatten the balls a bit with the back of a slightly moistened spoon or the bottom of a glass, sometimes dipped in sugar, to allow for more even baking. Cookies made by this method are apt to be of more uniform size and shape than drop cookies.

Planning Ahead

You can freeze cookie dough for 9 to 12 months. A convenient way to do this is to form the dough into a long roll or cylinder and seal it in heavy-duty aluminum freezer foil.

When you're ready to bake fresh cookies, thaw the dough, in its packaging, to room temperature. Preheat the oven, then slice ⅜-inch slabs off the roll and bake as directed in the recipe.

When packaging for freezing, be sure to wrap in a little piece of paper with baking directions in case you forget which recipe you used. Whip out a roll to warm the hearts of unexpected guests or to salvage the evening meal some night when everything else is ho-hum.

Be sure to allow enough room between cookies on the baking sheets so that everything doesn't run together. If the dough seems a bit softer than usual, leave extra room. You'll need even more generous spacing for larger cookies. About 2 inches apart is right for most kinds of 2- to 3-inch cookies.

While one batch of cookies is in the oven baking, leave the additional dough in the refrigerator. This keeps it cool (and also keeps it safe from marauders).

Step 9: Baking the Cookies

You may think that you've done all the work, and now you can clean up the kitchen and relax or move on to other things. But this is not the time to be casual! Of all the things you bake, butter cookies are one of the most easily burnt.

When you remove the baking sheets from the oven, the cookies will be very soft and fragile. Allow them to stand on the pans and set for a minute or two before removing them to racks to cool. Cookies continue to bake from their own heat as well as from the heat of the pans. After a minute or two, carefully remove the cookies to racks. If you've used baking parchment, simply slide the whole thing off onto the racks. Otherwise, use a wide, flexible spatula that holds the entire cookie.

If you're reusing the pans for another batch of cookies, be sure the pans are completely cool. Warm pans will cause the cookies to run and spread, and thus possibly to burn. Scrape any crumbs from the first batch off the tray, and regrease or reline the tray, if necessary, before loading on the next batch.

Most of the recipes that follow have an approximate yield noted, but this, of course, depends on how large you make your cookies. It also depends on how much raw dough has been snitched before it ever makes it to the pans!

AVOIDING
BREAKUPS

It's especially easy to break crisp cookies when they're fresh from the oven. If thin, crisp cookies stick to the pans, put them back in the oven briefly, melting them just enough to allow them to slip free.

Tips for Avoiding Burned Cookies

- **Use an oven thermometer** to be sure your oven is at the correct temperature; 8 to 10 minutes of cooking time doesn't leave much margin for error in oven temperature.

- **Always set your timer** the moment you close the oven door and the cookies begin baking, and always set it for the shorter amount of time suggested in the recipe. Even so, try to remember to check how everything is going a minute or two before the baking time is up.

- **Halfway through baking time,** switch the baking sheets around in the oven: Move the top sheet to the bottom and vice versa, and while you're at it, turn them front to back. If you were to move your thermometer around in the oven, you would be surprised by the temperature differences in various areas. Rotating the baking sheets helps compensate for these differences and ensure even browning. Convection ovens bake cookies faster, but the heat is still uneven; be sure to turn the sheets in these ovens as well.

- **Let your nose as well as your timer** be your guide. One of the best parts about baking chocolate chip cookies is the wonderful aroma that fills your home — almost reason enough to undertake the project! Be conscious of that delicious smell, and you'll be alert to any change that signals overbrowned butter or sugar.

Step 10: Storing the Cookies

Storage seems to be a rare problem for chocolate chip cookie bakers: The cookies disappear before there's a chance of their getting stale! In fact, some people feel the only way to ensure safe storage for some special event is to guard them with your life, while others attach to the cookie jar warnings, such as, "Hands Off!" or, more effective still, "You touch, you die!"

Tricks For
Fresh Taste

- If cookies are dry, place them in a plastic bag with a piece of bread or a slice of apple.

- Refresh stale cookies by placing them on baking sheets in a 300°F oven for a few minutes or by placing them on a paper towel and microwaving for 15 or 20 seconds.

But if you do get to stash any cookies away, be sure that you store them in airtight containers. If you use plastic containers, you may wish to put the cookies into plastic bags first to keep the cookies from picking up a petroleum-like smell from the container. Some cooks prefer to use lined cookie tins rather than plastic. If the cookies are particularly soft or sticky, place sheets of waxed paper between layers to prevent them from sticking together, especially in warmer weather. Don't try to store two different-flavored cookies in the same container; they'll absorb flavors from one another and lose their own distinctive tastes.

Almost all chocolate chip cookies freeze extremely well. This is one sneaky way to make them a little harder to get at! On the other hand, many folks just love frozen, unthawed cookies, especially for "dunking." To achieve a fresh-baked taste and texture, place frozen cookies in the microwave oven for 15 or 20 seconds before serving.

Freeze your cookies in airtight, rigid containers to keep them from getting broken. If you use a tin of some sort, line it first with a plastic bag to assure airtightness. Place sheets of waxed paper between layers to cushion the cookies. Thaw at room temperature, in the packaging, so that the cookies don't become soggy.

Striking Off on Your Own

In the pages that follow, you'll find more than 100 chocolate chip cookie recipes to try out. These may inspire you to invent your own special recipe, one that suits your personal opinion of how cakey and soft, or crisp and chewy, you think a chocolate chip cookie should be. Here are some tips to guide your choices.

Butter, margarine, and shortening. The higher the proportion of butter, margarine, or shortening to the other ingredients, the chewier, moister, and thinner your cookies will be.

Butter: Improves flavor; makes a crisp cookie; is more expensive; spreads and causes cookies to burn more easily

Margarine: Improves texture

Shortening: Stores for a longer period

Sweetener. You can use white or brown sugar or both. Some people believe that if you substitute a tablespoon or two of corn syrup or honey for some of the sugar, you'll get a chewier cookie without having to undercook the dough. Be sure to reduce any other liquid in the dough to compensate for the added liquid in these sweeteners.

Sugar: Makes cookies tender

Corn syrup: Makes chewy cookies with a crisp outside

Honey: Makes moist, soft cookies

Eggs contribute to the cookies' moisture, and they also make cookies light and tender. Additional egg yolk will pro-duce a cakier cookie.

Flavor. Use vanilla extract or any other flavor you prefer — for example, almond, peppermint, orange, or lemon.

Flour. Combine all-purpose flour with whole wheat flour for a more interesting texture. Or use more flour: The more you use in proportion to the butter-sugar mixture, the thicker and cakier the cookie will be.

All-purpose flour: Makes cookies light

Whole-wheat flour: Makes cookies denser

Cake flour: Creates a crumbly texture

Bread flour: May create a tough cookie

Leavening. Both baking powder and baking soda help make tender cookies; baking soda increases the tenderness.

Chocolate involves finesse. There are those, of course, who would never believe you could have too much chocolate in a cookie, but you're baking cookies after all, not making candy! Nestlé has actually surveyed consumers to estimate preferences. Over half of those questioned thought the ideal cookie should contain 6 to 10 chips, and only 12 percent wanted 20 or more chips in each cookie. Your only concern, of course, is the size of the "chocolate tooth" of those for whom you are baking.

Baking time and temperature. The average cookie baking time and temperature is about 10 minutes in a 350–375°F oven. If you like harder cookies, bake them longer, at a lower temperature (say 300–325°F for 15 to 20 minutes). For soft, chewy cookies, bake at high heat for a shorter period of time (400°F for 6 to 8 minutes).

Experiment and enjoy! Remember, chocolate chip cookies are practically impossible to spoil.

The Orchards' Chocolate-Chocolate Chip Cookies

To transform these cookies into peanut butter chocolate-chocolate chip, pastry chef Heather Andrus adds about 1 cup peanut butter to this recipe. The peanut butter should be creamed with the margarine before the sugars are added.

The Orchards 🍫 Williamstown, Massachusetts

5¼ cups flour

1 cup plus 2 tablespoons unsweetened cocoa

2¼ teaspoons baking soda

½ teaspoon salt

2½ cups margarine

2 cups granulated sugar

1¾ cups brown sugar, firmly packed

5 eggs

1½ teaspoons vanilla extract

2½ cups chocolate chips

1. Preheat the oven to 350°F.

2. Sift together the flour, cocoa, baking soda, and salt, and set the mixture aside.

3. In a large bowl, cream the margarine with a wooden spoon. Gradually beat in the granulated and brown sugars, creaming until well blended. Beat in the eggs, one at a time, and the vanilla. Stir in the dry ingredients, combining them well with your hands to avoid overmixing. Add the chocolate chips.

4. Drop the dough by heaping tablespoonfuls onto parchment-lined cookie sheets. Bake for about 8 minutes. Do not overcook. Place the baking sheet on a rack so that air can circulate under the cookies as they cool, or slide parchment paper, with the cookies still in place, onto racks to cool. When they're completely cool, store them tightly covered.

Yield: 9 to 9½ dozen

The Orchards' Chocolate Chip Cookies

The classic cookie for every classic occasion.

The Orchards 🍫 *Williamstown, Massachusetts*

6 cups flour

1 tablespoon baking soda

1 tablespoon salt

3 cups margarine

2½ cups brown sugar, firmly packed

1 cup granulated sugar

5 eggs

2 teaspoons vanilla extract

2½ cups semisweet chocolate chips

1. Preheat the oven to 350°F.

2. Combine the flour, baking soda, and salt, and set the mixture aside.

3. In a large bowl, cream the butter with a large wooden spoon. Add the brown and granulated sugars and continue creaming until they're well blended. Beat in the eggs, one at a time, and the vanilla. Mix in the dry ingredients, using your hands to blend them well. Gently stir in chocolate chips.

4. Drop by heaping tablespoonfuls onto parchment-lined cookie sheets. Bake for about 8 minutes. Do not overcook. Place the baking sheet on a rack so that air can circulate under the cookies as they cool, or slide parchment paper, with the cookies still in place, onto racks to cool. When they're completely cool, store them tightly covered.

Yield: 9 to 9½ dozen

THE COOKIES

The Winners

The judges of the Orchards' 1987 contest were three editors from *Chocolatier* magazine; Orchards pastry chef Heather Andrus; and the owners of the inn, Chester and Carol Soling. Each judge had 3 minutes to savor each cookie and rank it on a scale of 1 to 10. Sips of cold milk, water, or champagne cleared their palates for the next tasting.

After the tasting, the contest judges selected the winners.

TRADITIONAL
Chocolate Chip Cookies

Some people just like the classics. After all, it's pretty hard to beat the Original Toll House cookie invented by Ruth Wakefield in the early '30s. Change the recipe proportions a little, choose margarine or shortening instead of butter, though, and you've got a whole new cookie.

The recipes starting on page 41 have some extra twists that move them beyond the "plain chocolate chip cookie." It's that dash of almond flavoring, corn syrup instead of sugar, oil replacing butter, different-flavored chips, or some dried fruit that gives them a personality all their own. Everybody has a fantasy of *the* chocolate chip cookie: One of these might be just right for you.

Richard's Chocolate Chip Cookies

*Butter gives these classic cookies a rich flavor and crisp texture.
Be sure to use margarine to grease the baking sheets, however,
since butter can cause the cookies to burn on the bottom.*

Richard MacDonald 🍫 Chadds Ford, Pennsylvania

1 cup plus 2 tablespoons
flour

½ teaspoon baking soda

½ teaspoon salt

½ cup butter

6 tablespoons granulated
sugar

6 tablespoons brown
sugar, firmly packed

1 egg

½ teaspoon vanilla extract

½ cup chopped nuts
(optional)

6 ounces (1 cup) semi-
sweet chocolate chips or
semisweet chocolate bar
cut into pea-sized pieces

1. Preheat the oven to 350°F.

2. Sift the flour before measuring, then sift again with
the baking soda and salt; set aside.

3. In a large mixing bowl, cream the butter. Add the
sugars gradually, and continue beating until the mixture is creamy. Beat in the egg and vanilla. Stir in the
sifted ingredients, then the nuts and chocolate chips.

4. Drop by teaspoonfuls onto greased baking sheets,
spacing cookies well apart. Bake for 8 to 10 minutes
or until golden brown.

Yield: about 3 dozen

Susan's Chocolate Chip Cookies

*Softer and chewier than most traditional chocolate chip cookies,
these cookies get their distinctive texture from the way
they're beaten with an electric mixer. Try freezing these cookies
and then dipping them in a cup of hot coffee.*

Susan S. Grossman 🍪 Canton, Ohio

3 cups flour

1 teaspoon baking soda

1 teaspoon salt

1 cup margarine, at room temperature

¾ cup granulated sugar

¾ cup light brown sugar, firmly packed

1 teaspoon vanilla

1 teaspoon water

2 eggs

18 ounces (3 cups) semi-sweet chocolate chips

1. Preheat the oven to 350°F.

2. Sift the flour before measuring, then sift again with the baking soda and salt; set aside.

3. In a large bowl, combine the margarine, sugars, vanilla, and water and beat with an electric mixer about 2 minutes, until creamy. Add the eggs and beat until fluffy.

4. While gradually adding the sifted ingredients, beat with the electric mixer for about 2 minutes, until very well blended.

5. Stir in the chocolate chips.

6. Drop by heaping teaspoonfuls onto lightly greased baking sheets. Bake on the middle oven rack for 10 to 12 minutes, or until the cookies are lightly browned and slightly crisp on the bottom. (They may seem slightly undercooked.) Do not overbake. Cool 1 minute on the baking sheets, then remove cookies to paper towels to cool completely.

Yield: about 5 dozen

Colleen's
Chocolate Chip Cookies

The two extra-large eggs in this recipe render these cookies moist, light, and tender.

Colleen Iermini   Santa Cruz, California

3 cups flour

1 teaspoon baking soda

1 teaspoon salt

1 cup margarine

1⅓ cups granulated sugar

⅔ cup light brown sugar, firmly packed

1½ teaspoons vanilla extract

2 extra-large eggs

18 ounces (3 cups) semi-sweet chocolate chips

1. Preheat the oven to 325°F.

2. Without sifting, combine the flour, baking soda, and salt; set aside.

3. In a large mixing bowl, cream the margarine with the sugars until light. Beat in the vanilla and eggs until the mixture is smooth. Beat the dry ingredients into the creamed mixture, a little at a time. Add the chocolate chips and stir to mix well.

4. Drop the dough by heaping tablespoonfuls onto parchment-lined baking sheets, spacing well apart. Bake for 12 minutes, turning the sheets about halfway through the baking time for even browning. Remove from the oven and slide the parchment off the sheets, with the cookies still on top. Leave undisturbed until the cookies are just barely cool enough to handle. Transfer to racks to cool completely.

Yield: about 4 dozen

Ric's Chocolate Chip Cookies

To get these cookies right, you have to roll up your sleeves and mix everything with your hands. These treats are particularly tasty dipped in a glass of cold milk.

Ric Traeger 🍪 *Fresno, California*

4½ cups flour

2 teaspoons baking soda

2 teaspoons salt

1½ cups granulated sugar

1½ cups brown sugar, firmly packed

2 cups shortening

3 eggs

2 teaspoons vanilla extract

12 ounces semisweet chocolate chips

1 cup chopped nuts

1. Preheat the oven to 375°F.

2. In a large mixing bowl, combine the flour, baking soda, salt, and sugars. Add the shortening, then squeeze and knead the dough thoroughly with your hands. Add the eggs and vanilla and continue to knead until the dough is firm. Add the chocolate chips and nuts.

3. Form 1-inch balls of dough and place them about 2 inches apart on ungreased baking sheets. Bake for 10 to 15 minutes, or until golden brown. Remove from the oven and allow to cool on the baking sheets for about 2 minutes. Then, with a spatula, transfer the cookies to wire racks to cool completely.

Yield: about 7 dozen

Beverly's
Chocolate Chip Cookies

Developed for the Flying Cloud Inn in New Marlboro,
Massachusetts, this traditional cookie can be made soft and chewy
or crisp and crumbly simply by regulating the baking time.

Beverly Langeveld   Lanesboro, Massachusetts

3 cups flour

1 teaspoon baking soda

½ teaspoon salt

1 cup butter, softened

1 cup brown sugar, firmly packed

½ cup granulated sugar

2 teaspoons vanilla extract

2 eggs

9 ounces (1½ cups) semi-sweet chocolate chips

1 cup chopped walnuts

1. Preheat the oven to 350°F.

2. Sift together the flour, baking soda, and salt; set aside.

3. In a large mixing bowl, cream together the butter, sugars, and vanilla until light. Add the eggs one at a time and mix until well blended. Add the sifted ingredients and mix until well combined. Add the chocolate chips and nuts and blend well.

4. Drop by heaping teaspoonfuls 2 inches apart onto well-greased baking sheets. Bake for 8 to 10 minutes, or until lightly browned for a chewy cookie or darker for a crisp one. Let stand on the baking sheets for 1 minute before removing to a cooling rack.

Yield: 6 to 7 dozen

Alexis's Chocolate Chip Cookies

For flat, crisp cookies, drop dough by teaspoonfuls onto baking sheets and pop them into the oven for about 10 minutes. If you prefer chewy cookies, try refrigerating the dough for a couple of hours and then forming it into balls for baking. To avoid stickiness, wet your hands while working with dough.

Alexis C. Ducat   Cherry Hill, New Jersey

1 cup unsalted (sweet) butter

1 teaspoon vanilla extract

1 teaspoon salt

1½ cups light brown sugar, firmly packed

½ cup granulated sugar

2 large eggs

1 teaspoon baking soda

1 teaspoon warm water

2¼ cups flour

24 ounces (4 cups) semi-sweet chocolate chips

2 cups walnut pieces

1. Preheat the oven to 375°F.

2. In a large mixing bowl, cream the butter. Add the vanilla, salt, and sugars, and beat until light and fluffy. Add the eggs and beat well.

3. Dissolve the baking soda in the warm water. Gradually add the baking soda mixture and flour to the creamed mixture, beating just until all the flour is blended in. Stir in the chocolate and walnuts. Do not overmix.

4. Drop by teaspoonfuls onto greased cookie sheets. Bake for about 10 minutes, until cookies are light brown.

Yield: 3 dozen

Mona's Chocolate Chip Cookies

Finalist

*Whether you choose butter or margarine,
Mona's recipe is sure to please. Remember that butter
will make the cookies crisp and margarine will make them cakey.*

Mona B. Spencer 🍫 Vancouver, Washington

2 cups plus 4 tablespoons flour

1 teaspoon baking soda

1 teaspoon salt

1 cup granulated sugar

½ cup brown sugar, firmly packed

2 eggs

1 teaspoon vanilla extract

1 cup butter or margarine, softened till almost melted

12 ounces (2 cups) semi-sweet chocolate chips

2 cups coarsely chopped walnuts (optional)

1. Preheat the oven to 375°F.

2. Sift the flour with the baking soda and salt. Add the sugars, eggs, vanilla, and butter or margarine, and beat with a wooden spoon until the mixture is smooth and well combined. Stir in the chocolate chips and nuts.

3. Drop by teaspoonfuls onto ungreased baking sheets, spacing cookies about 2 inches apart. Bake for 10 to 12 minutes, or until cookies are golden. Remove to wire racks to cool.

Yield: 4 dozen

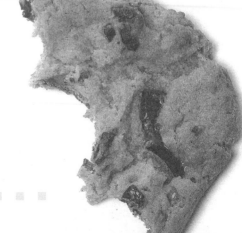

Chocolate Chip Cookies with Oil

The cookies from this old family recipe are soft and chewy, with a lovely golden tint. Though you may chill the dough before baking it, allow it to return to room temperature before putting the cookies in the oven. These cookies don't turn out as well if cooked in a convection oven.

Theresa R. Kennedy   Middleport, Ohio

3 cups flour

1 teaspoon baking soda

½ teaspoon salt

1 cup brown sugar

½ cup granulated sugar

1 cup vegetable oil (do not substitute butter, margarine, or shortening)

2 eggs

1 teaspoon vanilla extract

12 ounces (2 cups) semi-sweet chocolate chips

¾ cup chopped walnut pieces (optional)

1. Preheat the oven to 350°F.

2. Sift together the flour, baking soda, and salt; set aside.

3. Using an electric mixer, in a large bowl combine both the sugars and the oil thoroughly. Add the eggs and vanilla and beat well. Add the sifted ingredients to the creamed mixture, 1 cup at a time, beating the dough well after each addition of flour. Stir in the chocolate chips and nuts.

4. Drop by heaping teaspoonfuls onto ungreased baking sheets, spacing well apart. Bake for 7 to 8 minutes, or until golden.

Yield: about 5 dozen

Grandma's Chocolate Chip Cookies with Oil

A small amount of vegetable oil makes these nice-looking cookies especially crispy. The recipe is an adaptation of one given by a 1940s radio cook.

Thelma Laprey   Pawtucket, Rhode Island

1 cup plus 2 tablespoons flour

½ teaspoon baking soda

¼ teaspoon salt

¼ cup butter

¼ cup margarine

6 tablespoons granulated sugar

6 tablespoons brown sugar

1 egg

½ teaspoon vanilla extract

1 tablespoon corn oil

1 cup semisweet chocolate chips

½ cup chopped walnuts

1. Preheat the oven to 375°F.

2. Sift together the flour, baking soda, and salt; set aside.

3. In a large mixing bowl, cream together the butter, margarine, and sugars until fluffy. Add the egg, vanilla, and corn oil. Add the sifted ingredients to the creamed mixture, blending well. Stir in the chocolate chips and nuts.

4. Drop by teaspoonfuls onto ungreased baking sheets, spacing well apart. Bake for 8 to 10 minutes, or until light brown. Allow cookies to remain on the baking sheets about 2 minutes before removing to racks with a metal spatula to cool.

Yield: about 3 dozen

Nutty Chocolate Chip Cookies

*If you don't like chunks of nuts in your cookies,
here's a compromise: Grind the nuts finely
to get the flavor of nuts without the pieces.
Add an extra ¼ cup flour to make these cookies chewier.*

Pamela McCartney 🍪 *Champaign, Illinois*

2¼ cups flour
1 teaspoon baking soda
1 teaspoon salt
1 cup margarine
¾ cup sugar
2 eggs
¾ teaspoon vanilla extract
¼ teaspoon almond extract
1 cup semisweet chocolate chips
½ cup (or less) finely ground pecans (optional)

1. Preheat the oven to 350°F.
2. Sift together the flour, baking soda, and salt three times; set aside.
3. In a large mixing bowl, cream together the margarine, sugar, eggs, and vanilla and almond extracts. Stir sifted ingredients into the creamed mixture, along with the chocolate chips and pecans.
4. Drop by teaspoonfuls onto greased baking sheets, spacing well apart. Bake for 10 minutes.

Yield: about 4 dozen

Big-Batch Chip Cookies

*This excellent, large, soft cookie is an old family recipe,
rich in flavor, with more-generous-than-usual
amounts of butter and vanilla.*

Angeline Birdsall   Corning, New York

4 cups flour

1½ teaspoons baking soda

1¼ teaspoons salt

1½ cups butter, softened

1½ cups granulated sugar

¾ cup dark brown sugar,
firmly packed

3 large eggs

3 teaspoons vanilla extract

1 teaspoon almond extract
(optional)

12 ounces (2 cups) semi-
sweet chocolate chips

½ cup chopped walnuts or
pecans (optional)

½ cup coconut (optional)

1. Preheat the oven to 375°F.

2. Sift together the flour, baking soda, and salt;
set aside.

3. In a large mixing bowl, cream the butter, sugars, eggs,
and vanilla, along with the almond extract. Stir in
the sifted ingredients. Gently stir in the chocolate
chips and the nuts and coconut.

4. Drop by rounded tablespoonfuls onto greased baking
sheets, spacing well apart. Bake for 10 minutes, or
until edges of cookies turn golden. Do not overbake;
cookies will continue baking after being removed
from oven. Allow to set on baking sheets for a few
minutes before gently removing to racks to cool.

Yield: about 6 dozen

Oh-Yum Chocolate-Chip Factory Cookies

*Carol Joy, the 14-year-old creator of this recipe, makes up batches of
19 dozen cookies at a time for sale to local schools and businesses.
She calls her business the Oh-Yum Chocolate-Chip Factory,
and she has recently been joined in the enterprise
by her 10-year-old brother.*

Carol Joy Brendlinger   *Portland, Oregon*

1⅔ cups all-purpose flour

1½ cups whole-wheat flour

1 teaspoon baking soda

1 teaspoon salt

1 cup margarine or short-ening

1 cup granulated sugar

1 cup brown sugar

2 eggs

2 tablespoons hot water

2½ teaspoons vanilla extract

12 ounces (2 cups) semi-sweet chocolate chips

1 cup chopped nuts

1. Preheat the oven to 375°F.

2. Sift together the flours, baking soda, and salt; set aside.

3. In a large mixing bowl, cream the margarine or shortening and sugars. Add the eggs, hot water, and vanilla and beat until fluffy. Stir in the sifted ingredients. Gently add the chocolate chips and nuts.

4. Drop the dough by teaspoonfuls onto greased baking sheets, spacing well apart. Bake for 8 to 10 minutes, or until cookies are light brown.

Yield: 5 to 6 dozen

Three-Chip Chocolate Chip Cookies

This wonderful cookie — though pricey — looks and tastes great!

Barbara Lerch Northbrook, Illinois

2½ cups flour

1 teaspoon baking soda

½ teaspoon salt

½ cup butter or margarine, softened

½ cup shortening

1 cup light brown sugar

½ cup granulated sugar

2 eggs

2 tablespoons light corn syrup

2 tablespoons water

2 teaspoons vanilla extract

12 ounces (2 cups) semisweet chocolate chips

8 ounces white chocolate chips

7 ounces milk chocolate

6 ounces Lindt Milk Chocolate Bars, broken into squares

1. Combine the flour, baking soda, and salt; set aside.

2. In a large mixing bowl, cream together the butter or margarine, shortening, sugars, eggs, corn syrup, water, and vanilla; beat well. Add the dry ingredients to the creamed mixture and beat well. With a large wooden spoon, gently stir in all the chocolate pieces.

3. Chill the dough at least 1 hour.

4. Preheat the oven to 375°F.

5. With moistened hands, roll the dough into walnut-sized pieces, then place on baking sheets lined with aluminum foil. (Do not grease the foil.) Bake for 10 to 12 minutes, or until cookies are *very* lightly browned. Cool for about 2 minutes before removing cookies from baking sheets.

Yield: 3 to 4 dozen

Macadamia–Milk Chocolate Chip Cookies

Very large chips for very large cookies — for very large appetites!

Jan Deering 🍫 Wichita, Kansas

2¼ cups flour

1 teaspoon baking soda

½ teaspoon salt

1 cup margarine

¾ cup granulated sugar

¾ cup brown sugar, firmly packed

2 eggs

1½ teaspoons vanilla extract

2 cups large milk chocolate chips (such as Guittard)

¾ cup chopped macadamia nuts

½ cup flaked coconut

1. Preheat the oven to 375°F.

2. Sift together the flour, baking soda, and salt; set aside.

3. Cream the margarine. Gradually add the sugars and beat until fluffy. Add the eggs one at a time, mixing well after each addition. Stir in the vanilla. Add the sifted ingredients and beat until well blended. Stir in the milk chocolate chips, macadamia nuts, and coconut.

4. Drop by quarter-cupfuls onto ungreased baking sheets, spacing cookies 3 inches apart. Bake for 16 to 19 minutes, or until cookies are golden.

Yield: about 3 dozen

White Chocolate and Macadamia Nut Chippers

For a special treat, make 6-inch cookies and serve warm with ice cream. You can substitute 1 cup semisweet chocolate chips for 1 cup of the white chocolate chips, and use almonds instead of macadamias. The optional coconut is a special inspiration of Danita's 2-year-old son, who tossed in a handful when his mother wasn't looking.

Danita Yanniello   Burbank, California

2 cups flour

1 teaspoon baking soda

½ teaspoon salt

1 cup butter or margarine, softened

¾ cup granulated sugar

¾ cup brown sugar, firmly packed

1 egg

1 teaspoon vanilla extract

12 ounces (2 cups) white chocolate chips, or bulk white chocolate cut into ¼-inch chunks

½ cup macadamia nuts, coarsely chopped

½ cup coconut (optional)

1. Preheat the oven to 375°F.

2. In a large mixing bowl, combine the flour, baking soda, and salt; set aside. Beat the butter or margarine, sugars, and egg until fluffy. Stir in the dry ingredients and blend in the vanilla. Gently stir in the chocolate, nuts, and coconut.

3. Drop by tablespoonfuls onto ungreased baking sheets, spacing cookies a few inches apart. Bake for 8 to 10 minutes, or until cookies are golden brown. Cool slightly, then remove to wire racks to cool completely.

Yield: 2½ dozen

Dad's Favorite
Milk Chocolate Chip Cookies

Varying the nuts gives these cookies an entirely different flavor.

Karen Klooz Hunter 🍫 *Hay Springs, Nebraska*

6 cups flour

1½ teaspoons baking soda

1½ teaspoons salt

2 cups butter

2½ cups brown sugar, firmly packed

1 cup granulated sugar

3 eggs

2 tablespoons vanilla extract

3 cups semisweet chocolate chips

3 cups milk chocolate chips

2 cups chopped pecans (or 1 cup pecans and 1 cup walnuts)

1. Preheat the oven to 350°F.

2. Sift together the flour, baking soda, and salt; set aside.

3. In a large mixing bowl, combine the butter, sugars, eggs, and vanilla, and cream thoroughly. Add the sifted ingredients to the creamed mixture and blend well. Stir in the chocolate chips and nuts.

4. Shape into balls. Place on cookie sheets and bake for 7 to 9 minutes, or until sides are slightly browned but centers still look gooey. *Do not overbake.*

Yield: about 6 dozen

Cakey Chocolate Chip Cookies

These soft, cakelike cookies are delightful with afternoon tea or hot chocolate. To make the chocolate pieces, first chill the chocolate bars. Working with only one bar of chocolate at a time, break off pieces of chocolate into the dry bowl of your food processor. With the metal blade, pulsate the machine until the chocolate gets to the size you want; don't overprocess. The size of the pieces will vary.

Mary A. Christmann 🍫 Los Altos, California

3¼ cups flour

1 teaspoon baking soda

½ teaspoon salt

1 cup unsalted (sweet) butter, brought to room temperature

1¼ cups granulated sugar

3 eggs

1 cup milk

1 teaspoon vanilla extract

3 (4-ounce) bars semi-sweet chocolate, broken into small pieces

1. Preheat the oven to 375°F.

2. Sift together the flour, baking soda, and salt; set aside.

3. In a large mixing bowl, cream the butter and sugar. Add the eggs one at a time, beating well after each addition. Gradually add the sifted ingredients to the creamed mixture alternately with the milk. Add the vanilla. Beat with an electric mixer until well combined, scraping the bowl occasionally with a rubber spatula. Stir in the chocolate pieces by hand.

4. Drop by heaping tablespoonfuls onto greased baking sheets, spacing the cookies about 2 inches apart. If desired, press each cookie into a neat circle with a moistened fork. Bake on the middle oven rack for 12 to 14 minutes, or until edges of cookies are lightly browned. Cool thoroughly on wire racks, then store in a covered container.

Yield: about 5 dozen

Melt-in-Your-Mouth
Triple Chocolate Chip Cookies

These cookies are for serious chocolate lovers who like their cookies very sweet. Be sure to sift the flour before measuring; too much flour will make the cookies tough.

Marcella A. Scalf 🍫 San Antonio, Texas

1 cup flour

½ teaspoon baking soda

¼ teaspoon salt

½ cup unsalted (sweet) butter, slightly softened

½ cup dark brown sugar, firmly packed

¼ cup granulated sugar

1 egg

1 teaspoon vanilla extract

½ cup pecans, coarsely chopped

¾ cup semisweet chocolate chips

¾ cup milk chocolate chips

4 ounces white chocolate, cut into tiny cubes

1. Preheat the oven to 375°F.

2. Sift the flour before measuring, then sift again with the baking soda and salt; set aside.

3. In a large mixing bowl, cream the butter. Add the sugars and beat until smooth and fluffy. Add the egg and beat until smooth. Add the vanilla; beat until well blended.

4. With a wooden spoon, stir in sifted ingredients until blended. Stir in nuts and chocolate pieces.

5. Drop by teaspoonfuls onto greased baking sheets, using about 1 tablespoon of dough for each cookie and spacing about 2 inches apart. Bake on the center oven rack for 10 minutes, or until cookies are browned around the edges and nearly set, but still soft to the touch in the center. Using a metal spatula, carefully transfer the cookies to racks to cool completely. For additional batches, cool, clean, and re-grease the baking sheets.

6. Cookies store well for up to 1 week at room temperature in an airtight container.

Yield: about 4 dozen

Milk Chocolate Chip Cookies

*To ensure even baking, rotate the cookie sheets
halfway through the baking period, turning them front to back
and exchanging the sheets from the top to bottom oven racks.
These cookies freeze especially well.*

Kelly Lucarelli ● *Beaverton, Oregon*

3 cups flour

1 teaspoon baking soda

1 teaspoon salt

1 cup margarine

1⅓ cups granulated sugar

⅔ cup brown sugar

1½ teaspoons vanilla

2 extra-large eggs

1 2-ounce milk chocolate bar, grated

12 ounces (2 cups) semi-sweet chocolate chips

1 cup chopped walnuts, cashews, macadamias, or pecans

1. Preheat the oven to 325°F.

2. Without sifting, mix the flour, baking soda, and salt; set aside.

3. In a large mixing bowl, cream the margarine with the sugars until light. Beat in the vanilla and eggs until the mixture is smooth. Add the grated chocolate bar.

4. Beat the dry ingredients into the creamed mixture. Add the chocolate chips and nuts, and stir to mix thoroughly.

5. Drop onto ungreased baking sheets, 1 heaping tablespoonful at a time. Bake for about 12 minutes, or until golden brown.

Yield: 5 dozen

Crème de Menthe Chocolate Chunk Cookies

If you're in a hurry, spread the dough over the bottom of a
9 x 11-inch baking pan and bake at 350°F for 20 to 25 minutes,
or until lightly browned. When cool, cut into squares.

Mary Cramer   North Adams, Massachusetts

2 cups flour

1 teaspoon baking soda

¼–½ teaspoon salt

1 cup butter, softened

1 cup granulated sugar

½ cup brown sugar, firmly packed

2 teaspoons vanilla extract

2 eggs

8 ounces Swiss semisweet chocolate, cut into ½-inch chunks

1¼ cups chopped almonds (optional)

3 dozen pieces crème de menthe candy, cut into quarters

1. Combine the flour, baking soda, and salt; set aside.

2. In a large mixing bowl, beat the butter, sugars, vanilla, and eggs until light and fluffy. Blend in the dry ingredients. Stir in the chocolate chunks, the almonds, and the crème de menthe candy. Chill for 1 hour.

3. Remove from the refrigerator and allow to stand for 10 minutes.

4. Preheat the oven to 350°F.

5. Drop dough by heaping tablespoonfuls onto ungreased baking sheets, spacing cookies about 2 inches apart. Bake for 12 to 15 minutes, or until cookies are lightly browned. Do not overbake. Cool 2 minutes; remove from sheets and cool upside down on racks.

Yield: 3½ dozen

Chocolate and Peanut Butter Chip Cookies

Be sure both the chocolate and peanut butter chips are cool when you mix them into the batter; soft chips will lose their shape and begin to blend into the dough. For a soft cookie, avoid overbaking.

Mike Coley ✎ Fort Lauderdale, Florida
Deborah Ann Coley-Floyd ✎ Biloxi, Mississippi

2¾ cups flour

1 teaspoon baking soda

½ cup butter, softened

½ cup shortening

1 cup light brown sugar, firmly packed

½ cup granulated sugar

3 eggs

1½ teaspoons vanilla extract

1½ cups chopped walnuts

12 ounces (2 cups) semi-sweet chocolate chips

12 ounces (2 cups) peanut butter chips

1. Preheat the oven to 325°F.

2. Combine the flour and baking soda; set aside.

3. With an electric mixer, in a large bowl, cream together the butter and shortening. Gradually add the sugars. Add the eggs one at a time, beating well after each addition. Add the vanilla.

4. Stir in the dry ingredients and mix well. Add the walnuts and chocolate and peanut butter chips. Mix well with your hands; the batter will be stiff.

5. Drop by rounded tablespoonfuls onto well-greased baking sheets. Refrigerate the unused dough while batches are baking. Bake for 10 to 12 minutes, or until cookies are light brown. Do not overbake; cookies will continue to bake when removed from the oven.

Yield: about 5 dozen

Minty Nut and Raisin Chocolate Chip Cookies

The refreshing taste of mint chocolate combined with hearty raisins gives this otherwise traditional cookie a nice boost.

Edward S. Toomer ◆ Biloxi, Mississippi

1¼ cups all-purpose flour

½ teaspoon baking soda

½ teaspoon salt

½ cup butter or margarine

⅓ cup granulated sugar

⅓ cup brown sugar, firmly packed

1 egg

½ teaspoon vanilla extract

⅔ cup nuts (preferably pecans), coarsely chopped

⅔ cup mint-chocolate morsels

½ cup raisins

1. Preheat the oven to 350°F.

2. Sift together the flour, baking soda, and salt; set aside.

3. In a medium mixing bowl, cream the butter and sugars. Add the egg and vanilla; beat well. Add the sifted ingredients to the butter mixture. Gently mix in the nuts, mint-chocolate morsels, and raisins.

4. Drop by teaspoonfuls onto prepared baking sheets, spacing cookies about 2 inches apart. Bake for 10 minutes. Allow cookies to cool partially before removing to a rack.

Yield: 2 to 3 dozen

Old-Fashioned Apricot Chocolate Chip Cookies

Here's a recipe for people who enjoy cookies with a nice texture that are not overly sweet. The larger the apricot slices, the chewier the cookie.

Pat Kite ◈ Newark, California

1½ cups flour

¼ teaspoon baking soda

¼ teaspoon salt

⅓ cup plus 3 tablespoons margarine

1 cup brown sugar, firmly packed

1 egg, beaten

1 teaspoon vanilla extract

6 ounces dried apricots

½ cup chopped walnuts

6 ounces (1 cup) semi-sweet chocolate chips

1. Preheat the oven to 350°F.

2. Sift together the flour, baking soda, and salt; set aside.

3. In a large mixing bowl, cream the margarine. Add the sugar and mix thoroughly. Add the egg and vanilla; blend well. Add the sifted ingredients.

4. Cut the apricots into pieces with scissors, then add to the batter along with the nuts and chocolate chips.

5. Drop by teaspoonfuls onto greased baking sheets, spacing well apart. Bake for about 10 minutes, or until golden. Allow cookies to cool partially before removing to a rack.

Yield: 3½ dozen

Golden Raisin Chocolate Chip Cookies

The success of this cookie depends on golden raisins, which impart chewiness, moistness, and a slightly tart flavor.

Diane Buntrock   Gibsonia, Pennsylvania

2¼ cups flour

1 teaspoon baking soda

1 teaspoon salt

1 cup butter, softened

¾ cup granulated sugar

¾ cup brown sugar, firmly packed

1 teaspoon vanilla

2 eggs

12 ounces (2 cups) semi-sweet chocolate chips

1½ cups golden raisins

1. Preheat the oven to 375°F.

2. Combine the flour, baking soda, and salt; set aside.

3. In a large bowl, combine the butter, sugars, and vanilla and beat until creamy. Beat in the eggs. Gradually stir in the dry ingredients, mixing well. Stir in the chocolate chips and raisins.

4. Drop by rounded tablespoonfuls onto ungreased baking sheets, spacing well apart. Bake 10 to 13 minutes, or until golden brown.

Yield: 2½ dozen

Cuisine d'Or
Chocolate Chunk Cookies

One way to achieve crisp outsides and chewy centers is by under-cooking. But in this recipe, a small amount of corn syrup is substituted for some of the brown sugar, to create a chewy texture without softness or undercooking. Store these cookies in the refrigerator.

Marcy Goldman-Posluns ✦ Montreal, Quebec

2⅛ cups flour

¾ teaspoon baking soda

Pinch of salt

1 cup unsalted butter, slightly cooler than room temperature

1¾ cups minus 1½ tablespoons brown sugar, firmly packed

1½ tablespoons corn syrup

2 large eggs, at room temperature, lightly beaten

2 teaspoons vanilla extract

⅛ teaspoon almond extract

8 ounces Swiss milk chocolate, cut into small chunks

8 ounces Swiss semisweet chocolate, cut into small chunks

1. Mix the flour with baking soda and salt; set aside.

2. With an electric mixer, in a large bowl, cream the butter until softened. Add the sugar; cream until light and fluffy. Blend in the corn syrup, scraping the bowl often.

3. Blend in the lightly beaten eggs and the vanilla and almond extracts. If the mixture seems curdled or unhomogenous, add a bit of the flour mixture to bind it.

4. Stir the dry ingredients into the creamed mixture, scraping down the sides of the bowl occasionally. Gently stir in the chocolate pieces by hand.

5. Chill the batter for 20 minutes.

6. Preheat the oven to 350°F.

7. Line baking sheets with parchment paper.

8. Drop by rounded teaspoonfuls onto the parchment-lined baking sheets. Flatten the cookies very slightly. Bake for 12 minutes, or until cookies are lightly golden brown. Cool 1 minute on sheets, then remove to a cooling rack. Store in the refrigerator to preserve flavors.

Yield: 4 dozen

Joyous Chocolate Chip Cookies

Finalist

Here's another cookie with a crisp, firm outside and soft, chewy inside, achieved by using corn syrup along with the sugar.

Robin Joy Minnick 🍫 Donelson, Tennessee

3 cups flour

1 teaspoon baking soda

1 teaspoon salt

½ cup butter

¼ cup shortening

1 cup brown sugar, firmly packed

½ cup granulated sugar

1 teaspoon vanilla extract

2 eggs

1 tablespoon milk

3 tablespoons dark corn syrup

12 ounces (2 cups) semi-sweet chocolate chips

½ cup pecans, broken

1. Preheat the oven to 350°F.

2. Sift together the flour, baking soda, and salt; set aside.

3. In a large mixing bowl, cream the butter and shortening. Gradually add the sugars, and cream thoroughly.

4. Mix together the vanilla, eggs, milk, and corn syrup. Add to the creamed mixture, beating until blended. Gradually add the dry ingredients, mixing well. Add the chocolate chips and nuts.

5. Form the dough into small balls, or drop by teaspoonfuls onto greased baking sheets, spacing well apart. Bake for 7 to 10 minutes, or until cookies are golden brown with slightly darker edges. When touched with a fingertip, the cookies should retain a slight dimple but should not collapse.

Yield: about 4 dozen

Black Walnut Chocolate Chip Cookies

Black walnuts give this cookie its distinctive flavor.
If they're not available in your area, you can mail-order them.
One supplier is Sunnyland Farms, Inc.; call (800) 999-2488 to order
a catalog, or visit the on-line store at www.nutsandcandies.com.

Linda Johnson 🍪 McKeesport, Pennsylvania

3 cups flour

1¼ teaspoons baking soda

1 teaspoon baking powder

1 cup granulated sugar

1 cup brown sugar, firmly packed

1 cup shortening

2 eggs

2 teaspoons vanilla extract

2 tablespoons powdered buttermilk

½ cup water

18 ounces (3 cups) semi-sweet chocolate chips

1 cup chopped black walnuts

1. Preheat the oven to 400°F.

2. Sift together the flour, baking soda, and baking powder; set aside.

3. In a large mixing bowl, cream the sugars and shortening until smooth. Beat in the eggs and vanilla.

4. Mix the powdered buttermilk with the water until smooth. Add to the creamed mixture. Stir in the sifted ingredients until well blended. Add the chocolate chips and nuts, stirring until they are evenly mixed in.

5. Drop by tablespoonfuls onto greased baking sheets, spacing well apart. Bake for 10 to 12 minutes, or until golden brown.

Yield: about 5 dozen

TRADITIONAL
Chocolate Chip Cookies
PLUS

When plain chocolate chip cookies aren't quite enough, when you're looking for a bit more — or perhaps a lot less — crunch, when spiciness or fruitiness would hit the spot, or when a honey, molasses, or maple syrup enthusiast is close at hand, leaf through the following group of recipes for something sure to please.

Crispy Rice Chocolate Chip Cookies

If you like a light crunch to your cookies,
try this rice cereal variation.

Marie H. Jackson 🥄 Lexington, Kentucky

1¾ cups flour

1 teaspoon baking soda

½ teaspoon salt

1 cup butter or margarine, softened

¾ cup granulated sugar

¾ cup brown sugar, firmly packed

2 eggs

1 teaspoon vanilla extract

2 cups crisp rice cereal

6 ounces (1 cup) semi-sweet chocolate chips

1. Preheat the oven to 350°F.

2. Mix together the flour, baking soda, and salt; set aside.

3. In a large mixing bowl, combine the butter or margarine and sugars and beat until well blended. Add the eggs and vanilla and beat well. Add the dry ingredients, mixing until combined. Stir in the cereal and chocolate chips.

4. Drop by tablespoonfuls onto greased baking sheets, spacing well apart. Bake for about 10 minutes or until cookies are lightly browned. Cool on trays for about 1 minute, then remove to cooling racks.

Yield: about 3 dozen

Potato Chip
Chocolate Chip Cookies

*Try varying this recipe by substituting peanut butter chips
for some or all of the chocolate chips, or use rum
or lemon extract in addition to the vanilla.*

Derene Wilson 🍫 Clearlake, California

2 cups flour

1 teaspoon baking soda

1 cup butter or margarine

1 cup granulated sugar

1 cup light brown sugar,
firmly packed

2 eggs

1 teaspoon vanilla extract

2 cups potato chips,
coarsely crushed

6 ounces (1 cup) semi-
sweet chocolate chips

1 cup chopped nuts
(optional)

1. Preheat the oven to 350°F.

2. Mix together the flour and baking soda; set aside.

3. In a large mixing bowl, cream the butter, sugars, and eggs until smooth and well blended. Stir in the vanilla. Stir in the dry ingredients and mix well. Gently add the potato chips and chocolate chips, then add the nuts and mix well to distribute everything evenly.

4. Drop by teaspoonfuls onto ungreased baking sheets, spacing well apart. Bake for 10 to 12 minutes, or until golden brown.

Yield: about 4 dozen

Spicy Chocolate Chip Cookies

*Keep this richly spiced cookie tightly covered
to preserve its moistness.*

Linda Leatherman  Mulvane, Kansas

2 cups all-purpose flour
2 cups whole-wheat flour
4 teaspoons cinnamon
1 teaspoon baking soda
1 teaspoon salt
½ teaspoon ginger
½ teaspoon cloves
2 cups brown sugar
½ cup honey (optional)
1½ cups shortening
4 eggs
1 teaspoon vanilla extract
1 cup water
4 cups rolled oats
12 ounces (2 cups) or more
   semisweet chocolate
   chips
1 cup nuts (optional)

1. Preheat the oven to 350°F.

2. Sift together the flours, cinnamon, baking soda, salt, ginger, and cloves; set aside.

3. In a large mixing bowl, cream together the sugar, honey, and shortening. Add the eggs and the vanilla. Add the sifted ingredients to the creamed mixture. Add the water and rolled oats and mix well. Gently stir in the chocolate chips and nuts.

4. Drop by teaspoonfuls onto greased baking sheets, spacing well apart. Bake for 12 to 15 minutes, or until golden brown.

Yield: 6 dozen

Spicy Pumpkin Chocolate Chip Cookies

Steam or bake fresh pumpkin, purée it, then freeze it in plastic bags in 1-cup portions that can be readily thawed for use in this recipe for up to a year. You can substitute canned pumpkin puree for fresh.

Connie Cwynar 🍪 Cape Coral, Florida

2 cups flour

4 teaspoons baking powder

1 tablespoon cinnamon

½ teaspoon nutmeg

¼ teaspoon ginger

1 teaspoon salt

½ cup shortening

1 cup granulated sugar

2 large eggs, beaten

1 cup pumpkin puree

6 ounces (1 cup) semi-sweet chocolate chips

1. Preheat the oven to 350°F.

2. Sift together the flour, baking powder, cinnamon, nutmeg, ginger, and salt; set aside.

3. In a large mixing bowl, cream the shortening and gradually add the sugar. Add the beaten eggs and pumpkin and mix well. Blend in the sifted ingredients until well mixed. Add the chocolate chips.

4. Drop by teaspoonfuls onto greased baking sheets, spacing well apart. Bake on the top rack of the oven for 15 minutes.

Yield: about 4 dozen

Spicy Frostbite Chocolate Chip Cookies

These are a good choice when you need cookies to pack up and mail. When Sherlyn, the teenager who invented this recipe, went off to college, she liked to receive boxes of her creation from home.

Sherlyn B. Morrissette   Lyndonville, Vermont

2 cups flour

1 teaspoon baking soda

2 teaspoons cinnamon, divided

1 teaspoon ground ginger

¼ teaspoon salt

1 cup butter

1½ cups brown sugar, firmly packed

1 egg

1½ teaspoons vanilla extract

12 ounces (2 cups) semi-sweet chocolate chips

1 cup chopped pecans or walnuts

2 cups confectioners' sugar

1. Sift together the flour, the baking soda, 1½ teaspoons of the cinnamon, the ginger, and the salt. Set aside.

2. In a large mixing bowl, cream the butter. Add the brown sugar, egg, and vanilla and beat well. Add the sifted ingredients to the butter mixture. Gently stir in the chocolate and nuts.

3. Refrigerate overnight or until firm.

4. Preheat the oven to 350°F.

5. Form balls consisting of 1 tablespoon of dough.

6. Mix the remaining ½ teaspoon of cinnamon with the confectioners' sugar. Roll the balls in the sugar mixture and space about 2 inches apart on ungreased baking sheets. Bake for 15 minutes.

Yield: about 3 dozen

California Chocolate Chip Cookies

This not-too-sweet cookie has the sunshine taste of fresh oranges.

Libia Foglesong 🍪 San Bruno, California

3 cups flour

1 teaspoon baking soda

1 teaspoon salt

⅔ cup ground walnuts

1 cup margarine, softened

1 cup dark brown sugar, firmly packed

¾ cup granulated sugar

2 teaspoons vanilla extract

2 large eggs

1 tablespoon orange juice

1½ tablespoons finely chopped orange zest

18 ounces (3 cups) semi-sweet chocolate chips

1½ cups coarsely chopped walnuts

1. Preheat the oven to 350°F.

2. Sift together the flour, baking soda, and salt. Mix in the ground walnuts and set aside.

3. In a large mixing bowl, cream the margarine with the sugars until the mixture is light and fluffy. Add the vanilla, eggs, orange juice, and orange zest, and beat until smooth. Add the sifted ingredients and mix until completely blended. Add the chocolate chips and chopped walnuts; stir to distribute evenly.

4. Form the dough into balls a bit larger than walnuts, or drop by tablespoonfuls onto parchment-lined baking sheets. Bake for about 10 minutes, just until cookies are a very light golden color. With a spatula, transfer the cookies to cooling racks.

Yield: 4½ dozen

Taste-of-Summer Chocolate Chip Cookies

*Peach schnapps, a hint of almond, the nutlike wholesomeness
of rolled oats — and chocolate, of course:
These cookies are like a breath of summer air.*

Linda J. Kick 🍫 Camillus, New York

2½ cups flour

1 teaspoon baking soda

1 teaspoon salt

1 cup butter or margarine, softened

¾ cup plus 2 tablespoons light brown sugar, firmly packed

¾ cup granulated sugar

2 eggs

1½ teaspoons vanilla extract

½ teaspoon almond extract

⅓ cup peach schnapps

12 ounces (2 cups) semi-sweet chocolate chips

1 cup quick-cooking rolled oats

1. Preheat the oven to 350°F.

2. Combine the flour, baking soda, and salt; set aside.

3. In a large mixing bowl, cream the butter and sugars. Add the eggs, vanilla and almond extracts, and schnapps and beat well. Gradually add the dry ingredients, blending well. Stir in the chocolate chips and oats.

4. Drop by rounded teaspoonfuls onto lightly greased baking sheets, spacing well apart. Bake for 10 to 12 minutes, or until cookies are very lightly browned. Remove from baking sheets to cool.

Yield: about 4 dozen

Orange Chocolate Chip Cookies

*Tangy orange and rich chocolate combine for a refreshing taste
of warm, exotic places. Be sure to chill the dough and baking sheets,
or the cookies will spread. Don't crowd the cookies, and rotate
the sheets in the oven partway through the baking period.*

Nancy G. Means   Moline, Illinois

2¼ cups flour

1 teaspoon salt

1 cup butter, softened

¾ cup light brown sugar, firmly packed

½ cup granulated sugar

¼ cup honey

2 eggs, at room temperature, beaten

1 teaspoon baking soda dissolved in 1 teaspoon hot water

1 tablespoon finely grated fresh orange zest

12 ounces (2 cups) semi-sweet chocolate minichips

1 teaspoon vanilla extract

1 cup chopped nuts (optional)

1. Sift the flour before measuring, then sift again with the salt; set aside.

2. With an electric mixer, cream the butter and sugars in a large bowl until the mixture is light, fluffy, and pale yellow. Blend in the honey. Add the beaten eggs. Continue to beat on medium speed for about 2 minutes.

3. Add the dissolved baking soda. Gradually add the sifted ingredients, beating well after each addition. Stir in the orange peel, chocolate chips, vanilla, and nuts. Chill the dough for 1 hour.

4. Preheat the oven to 350°F.

5. Drop by rounded teaspoonfuls onto chilled, lightly greased baking sheets, spacing well apart. With the bottom of a glass dipped lightly in granulated sugar, flatten the cookies slightly to prevent sticking. Bake 10 to 12 minutes, or until cookies are lightly browned. Cool on wire racks.

Yield: about 3 dozen

Apricot Chocolate Chip Cookies

The dried apricots for this recipe should be plump, moist, and tender. If you're stuck with brown, shriveled, and brittle fruit, be sure to simmer the apricots in water until they've softened before using. Save the cooking water and add it to juice, gelatin, or sliced fruit. For a soft, chewy cookie, bake for about 8 minutes; if you prefer a crisp, hard cookie for dunking, bake a bit longer.

Gina M. Glick 🍫 Carrollton, Texas

1½ cups flour

1¼ teaspoons baking powder

¼ cup dried apricots

⅓ cup butter, softened

⅔ cup granulated sugar

1 egg

6 tablespoons apricot preserves

6 ounces (1 cup) semi-sweet chocolate chips

1. Preheat the oven to 375°F.

2. Sift together the flour and baking powder; set aside.

3. Chop or snip the dried apricots into pieces slightly smaller than the chips. Cover them with boiling water and set aside.

4. In a large mixing bowl, blend the butter and sugar until the mixture is light and creamy. Add the egg and the apricot preserves and continue to beat until well blended. Pieces of apricot will remain visible.

5. Stir the sifted ingredients into the creamed mixture until it is well blended. Fold in the chocolate chips.

6. Drain the water from the apricot bits and fold them into the batter.

7. Drop batter by teaspoonfuls onto ungreased baking sheets, spacing cookies about 2 inches apart. Bake for 8 to 12 minutes, or until edges of cookies are slightly brown.

Yield: 3 dozen

Grandma Matthews's Molasses Chocolate Chip Cookies

*Grandma Matthews's family recipe is well over 100 years old.
Grandma, who firmly believed in the benefits of blackstrap molasses,
kept a jug of it on the table, and used quantities in all her baking.*

Edith Stacey   Fitchburg, Massachusetts

2½ cups flour, sifted

1 teaspoon baking powder

½ teaspoon salt

¾ cup butter

¾ cup granulated sugar

¾ cup brown sugar, firmly packed

1 egg, well beaten

¼ cup molasses

1 teaspoon vanilla extract

3 tablespoons milk

6 ounces (1 cup) semi-sweet chocolate chips

½ cup chopped walnuts

1. Preheat the oven to 325°F.
2. Sift the flour with the baking powder and salt; set aside.
3. Cream the butter with the sugars until the mixture is light and fluffy. Add the egg and molasses.
4. Stir the vanilla into the milk, and add to the butter mixture alternately with the sifted ingredients. Gently stir in the chocolate chips and nuts.
5. Drop by teaspoonfuls onto ungreased baking sheets, spacing well apart. Bake for 10 to 12 minutes, or until golden brown.

Yield: 4 dozen

Apple Orchard Chocolate Chippers

*The apple butter in these cookies adds a delicious spiciness
and also helps keep them moist.*

Shirley DeSantis 🍪 *East Windsor, New Jersey*

½ cup butter or
  margarine

½ cup granulated sugar

¼ cup brown sugar,
  firmly packed

1 egg

1 teaspoon vanilla
  extract

¼ cup apple butter

1½–2 cups unbleached
  flour, divided

½ teaspoon baking soda

½ teaspoon salt

6 ounces (1 cup) semi-
  sweet chocolate chips

1 apple, cored and
  shredded

1½ cup nuts (optional)

1. Preheat the oven to 350°F.

2. In a large mixing bowl, cream the butter or margarine, sugars, egg, and vanilla until light and fluffy. Add the apple butter and mix well.

3. Add 1 cup of the flour, the baking soda, and the salt, and mix until well blended. Gradually add the remaining flour, just until the dough is no longer wet and sticky. Stir in the chocolate chips, shredded apple, and nuts.

4. Drop the dough by teaspoonfuls onto lightly greased baking sheets, spacing cookies about 2 inches apart. Bake for 12 to 15 minutes, or until golden brown. Transfer to a cooling rack.

Yield: 3 to 4 dozen

Honey Chocolate Chip Cookies

Because honey retains and absorbs moisture, it's a great substitute for sugar when you want cookies that will not dry out. When substituting honey for sugar in other recipes, use three quarters as much honey as the amount listed for sugar, and reduce the other liquids in the recipe by ¼ cup for each cup of honey. This recipe was first published by the Nova Scotia Department of Agriculture and Marketing in a small booklet called Honey Recipes.

Alice Marum 🍂 Kingston, Nova Scotia

1 cup flour

1 teaspoon baking powder

¼ teaspoon salt

½ cup shortening

½ cup honey

1 small egg

½ teaspoon vanilla extract

½ cup semisweet chocolate chips

¼ cup nuts, chopped

1. Preheat the oven to 375°F.

2. Sift the flour before measuring, then sift twice with the baking powder and salt. Set aside.

3. In a large mixing bowl, cream the shortening and honey until the mixture is light and fluffy. Add the egg and beat well. Add the sifted ingredients to the shortening mixture. Add the vanilla and blend well. Fold in the chocolate chips and nuts. Chill.

4. Drop by teaspoonfuls onto greased baking sheets, spacing well apart. Bake for 12 minutes.

Yield: 2 dozen

Maple-Walnut Chippers

Maple syrup gives these chocolate chip cookies
a definite New England flavor.

Danita Yanniello  *Burbank, California*

2¼ cups flour

1 teaspoon baking soda

½ teaspoon salt

1 cup butter or margarine, at room temperature

½ cup granulated sugar

½ cup brown sugar, firmly packed

¼ cup maple syrup

1 egg

½ cup walnuts, coarsely chopped

12 ounces (2 cups) semi-sweet chocolate chips

1. Preheat the oven to 375°F.

2. Mix together the flour, baking soda, and salt; set aside.

3. In a large mixing bowl, cream together the butter, sugars, maple syrup, and egg. Add the dry ingredients, then mix until blended. Stir in the nuts and chocolate chips.

4. Drop by teaspoonfuls onto ungreased baking sheets, spacing well apart. Bake for 8 to 10 minutes, or until cookies are golden brown. Cool for a few minutes on the sheets, then remove cookies to a cooling rack.

Yield: 5 dozen

Black-and-White Cookies

To keep these soft, coconut chocolate chip cookies moist,
place them in a tightly covered container with a slice of bread.

Amy Garrett Prescott Valley, Arizona

1¾ cups flour

½ cup unsweetened cocoa

1 teaspoon baking soda

½ teaspoon salt

1 cup butter, at room temperature

1 cup brown sugar, firmly packed

⅓ cup granulated fructose

1½ teaspoons vanilla extract

2 eggs

12 ounces (2 cups) milk chocolate chips

⅔ cup sweetened flaked coconut

1. Preheat the oven to 350°F.

2. Combine the flour, cocoa, baking soda, and salt; set aside.

3. In a large bowl, beat the butter, sugar, fructose, and vanilla with an electric mixer on medium speed, until fluffy. Beat in the eggs until batter is well blended. On low speed, gradually mix in the dry ingredients just until well blended. With a wooden spoon, stir in the chips and coconut.

4. Drop the dough by heaping tablespoonfuls onto ungreased baking sheets, spacing well apart. Bake for 10 to 12 minutes, or until golden brown. Cool on the sheets for about 1 minute, then remove to racks to complete cooling.

Yield: 3½ dozen

Coconut Chocolate Chip Cookies

The mild flavor of coconut is the perfect complement for chocolate chips and pecans. For best results, do not skimp on the chocolate — this recipe loads every cookie with plenty of chocolate chips.

Bridget McDonough 🍫 Chicago, Illinois

2½ cups flour

1 teaspoon baking soda

1 teaspoon salt

¾ cup plus 2 tablespoons butter

2 tablespoons canned coconut cream

1 cup brown sugar, firmly packed

½ cup granulated sugar

2 eggs

1 teaspoon vanilla extract

2½ cups semisweet chocolate chips

1½ cups chopped pecans

½ cup sweetened flaked coconut

1. Preheat the oven to 375°F.

2. Combine the flour, baking soda, and salt; set aside.

3. In a large bowl, cream the butter and coconut cream. Add the sugars and beat until well mixed. Add the eggs and vanilla and beat until the mixture is creamy. Stir the dry ingredients into the creamed mixture just until completely blended in. Stir in the chocolate chips, pecans, and coconut until they are combined.

4. Drop by rounded tablespoonfuls onto greased baking sheets, spacing well apart. Bake for 8 to 9 minutes, or until golden brown.

Yield: 5 dozen

Agnes's Sour Cream Chocolate Chip Cookies

*If you're looking for a deliciously rich cookie
that just melts in your mouth, this is definitely it.*

Agnes M. Laflin   Tempe, Arizona

- 2 cups flour
- 1 teaspoon baking soda
- 1 teaspoon salt
- 1 cup butter or margarine, softened
- 1 cup granulated sugar
- ½ cup brown sugar, firmly packed
- 2 eggs
- 2 teaspoons vanilla extract
- ⅓ cup sour cream
- 1 cup chopped nuts
- 12 ounces (2 cups) semi-sweet chocolate chips

1. Preheat the oven to 350°F.
2. Sift together the flour, baking soda, and salt; set aside.
3. In a large mixing bowl, combine the butter, sugars, eggs, and vanilla, and beat until creamy. Stir in the sour cream and blend well. Add the sifted ingredients and blend well. Add the nuts and chocolate chips.
4. Drop by teaspoonfuls onto ungreased baking sheets, spacing well apart. Bake for 8 to 10 minutes, or until golden brown.

Yield: about 4 dozen

Tricia's Sour Cream Chocolate Chip Cookies

*Because these cookies have a cakelike texture, the sugar
doesn't carmelize and the cookies don't brown
the way other chocolate chip cookies do.*

Tricia Malanka   Pacific Grove, California

2–2½ cups flour, divided

1 teaspoon baking powder

½ teaspoon baking soda

Dash of salt

¾ cup plus 2 tablespoons granulated sugar

½ cup butter or margarine, melted

1 egg

½ cup sour cream

1 teaspoon vanilla extract

12 ounces (2 cups) semisweet chocolate chips

1. Preheat the oven to 375°F.

2. Sift together 1 cup of the flour and the baking powder, baking soda, and salt; set aside.

3. In a large mixing bowl, cream together the sugar and butter or margarine. Add the egg and mix well. Add the sour cream; mix until the mixture is smooth and no lumps of sour cream appear. Add the vanilla. Stir the sifted ingredients into the butter and sugar mixture. Add the remaining flour gradually, until a semi-firm but smooth consistency is obtained.

4. Add the chocolate chips and mix well.

5. Drop by teaspoonfuls onto greased baking sheets, spacing well apart. Bake for 12 to 15 minutes, or until cookies are *lightly* golden. Remember, these cookies will not brown, so be careful not to overbake.

Yield: 4 to 6 dozen

Yogurt and Pecan Chocolate Chip Cookies

A cakey, pecan-packed, chocolate-filled delight, these cookies are best served very fresh. Yogurt accounts in part for their distinctive flavor and cakelike texture.

Lisa De Mauro 🍫 Yonkers, New York

1¾ cups flour

¾ teaspoon baking soda

¼ teaspoon salt

½ cup unsalted (sweet) butter, at room temperature

1 cup plus 2 tablespoons sugar

2 tablespoons molasses

1½ teaspoons vanilla extract

1 large egg

½ cup plain, whole-milk yogurt

¾ cup broken pecan pieces

1½ cups semisweet chocolate chips

1. Preheat the oven to 350°F.

2. Sift the flour before measuring, then sift again with baking soda and salt; set aside.

3. In a large mixing bowl, cream the butter until it is fluffy. Add the sugar, beating until well blended. Add the molasses, vanilla, and egg and blend thoroughly. Add about 1 cup of the sifted ingredients and mix well. Blend in the yogurt. Add the remaining sifted ingredients, stirring to blend thoroughly. Stir in the nuts and chocolate chips.

4. Drop by rounded tablespoonfuls, spacing well apart, onto baking sheets lined with lightly greased aluminum foil. Bake for about 12 minutes, or until cookies are just turning golden brown. Remove from baking sheets to cool.

Yield: about 2½ dozen

Mocha Dreams

Coffee and chocolate have a natural affinity, and this recipe for eggless, coffee-flavored cookies capitalizes on the mutual attraction. Because these cookies don't spread, they're a good choice when you need a lot of small, bite-sized treats.

Barbara Nowakowski ◆ *North Tonawanda, New York*

2½ cups flour

½ teaspoon baking powder

¼ teaspoon salt

1 cup unsalted (sweet) butter

1 cup brown sugar

1 teaspoon vanilla extract

1 tablespoon instant coffee granules

12 ounces (2 cups) semi-sweet chocolate chips

1 cup chopped pecans or walnuts

1. Preheat the oven to 350°F.

2. Sift together the flour, baking powder, and salt; set aside.

3. In a large mixing bowl, cream together the butter and brown sugar. Blend in the vanilla and coffee granules. Add the sifted ingredients to the creamed mixture and blend well. Stir in the chocolate and the nuts.

4. Drop by teaspoonfuls onto lightly buttered baking sheets, spacing well apart. Bake at 350°F for 8 to 10 minutes, or until cookies are lightly browned. Cool slightly before removing from baking trays.

Yield: about 5 dozen

Pudding and Sweet Chocolate Chips

The secret ingredient of these cakelike cookies is instant pudding mix.

Joan Lehman  Columbus, Ohio

2¼ cups flour

1 teaspoon baking soda

1 cup butter, softened

¾ cup light brown sugar, firmly packed

¼ cup granulated sugar

1 teaspoon vanilla extract

1 package (four-serving size) instant vanilla pudding

2 eggs

2 bars (4 ounces) sweet baking chocolate, broken into small pieces

1. Preheat the oven to 350°F.

2. Mix the flour with the baking soda; set aside.

3. In a large mixing bowl, combine the butter, sugars, vanilla, and pudding mix, and beat until smooth and creamy. Beat in the eggs. Gradually add the dry ingredients. Gently stir in the chocolate pieces.

4. Drop by rounded teaspoonfuls onto ungreased baking sheets, spacing cookies about 2 inches apart. Bake for 15 to 20 minutes, or until golden brown.

Yield: about 5 dozen

Milk Chocolate Chip Delights

This melt-in-your-mouth cookie features milk chocolate morsels.

Betty Landers ❦ *Morganton, North Carolina*

2½ cups flour, unsifted

1 teaspoon baking soda

1 cup margarine, softened

¾ cup light brown sugar, firmly packed

¼ cup granulated sugar

1 teaspoon vanilla extract

1 package (four-serving size) instant vanilla pudding mix

2 eggs

12 ounces (2 cups) milk chocolate morsels

1. Preheat the oven to 375°F.

2. Sift together the flour and baking soda; set aside.

3. In a food processor, combine the margarine, sugars, vanilla, and pudding mix until the mixture is smooth and creamy. Beat in the eggs. Gradually blend in the sifted ingredients; the batter will be stiff. Gently stir in the chocolate morsels.

4. Drop by rounded teaspoonfuls onto ungreased baking sheets, spacing cookies about 2 inches apart. Flatten a bit with the back of a fork; these cookies spread very little while baking. Bake for 8 to 10 minutes, or until golden brown.

Yield: about 5 dozen

Tiger-Striped Chocolate Chip Cookies

When you mix the melted chocolate chips into the dough, be careful not to overmix. The chocolate should be swirled in just enough to make stripes.

Sanna Techau 🍫 *Cynthiana, Kentucky*

2½ cups flour

1 teaspoon baking soda

¼ teaspoon salt

8 ounces tub margarine

½ cup creamy peanut butter

1 cup granulated sugar

1 cup brown sugar, firmly packed

2 eggs

1 teaspoon vanilla extract

1 (8-ounce) milk chocolate bar, cut into ¼- to ½-inch chunks

6 ounces (1 cup) semi-sweet chocolate chips

1. Preheat the oven to 350°F.

2. Sift together the flour, baking soda, and salt; set aside.

3. In a large mixing bowl, cream the margarine, peanut butter, and sugars until the mixture is light and fluffy. Beat in the eggs and vanilla. Add the sifted ingredients and mix well. Gently stir in the milk chocolate chunks.

4. In a saucepan, melt the chocolate chips over very low heat. Carefully stir the melted chocolate into the cookie dough to make stripes. Do *not* blend into the dough.

5. Drop by teaspoonfuls onto ungreased baking sheets, spacing well apart. Bake for 10 to 12 minutes, or until the light stripes are golden. Cool slightly before removing from baking sheets. Store in an airtight container.

Yield: 4 dozen

Keep Your Options Open

A little of this, a little more of that — vary this recipe to suit your mood!
For best results, however, don't substitute margarine for the butter.

Rose Kegler Hallarn 🍪 Columbus, Ohio

3 cups flour

1 teaspoon baking soda

1 teaspoon salt

⅓ cup shortening

1 cup butter, softened

1 cup granulated sugar

1 cup brown sugar, firmly packed

2 eggs

2 teaspoons vanilla extract

½ teaspoon coconut flavoring (optional)

½ teaspoon almond extract (optional)

1 cup chopped pecans or almonds (or a combination)

9–12 ounces (1½–2 cups) milk chocolate chips or semi-sweet chocolate chips

4–6 ounces (¾–1 cup) butter-scotch chips (optional)

1. Mix together the flour, baking soda, and salt; set aside.

2. In a large mixing bowl, beat the shortening, butter, sugars, and eggs until well blended. Add the vanilla, coconut flavoring, and almond extract. Gradually add the dry ingredients, a cup at a time, mixing well after each addition. Fold in the nuts and chips. Refrigerate for 2 hours or overnight.

3. Preheat the oven to 375°F.

4. Drop dough by teaspoonfuls onto greased baking sheets, spacing well apart. Bake for 12 to 14 minutes, or until golden brown. Cool on racks.

Option: For a special treat, roll teaspoon-sized balls of dough in a mixture of cinnamon and sugar (2 tablespoons of sugar to ½ tablespoon of cinnamon) before baking as directed above.

Yield: 4 to 5 dozen

Double Peanut Butter Chocolate Chip Cookies

You'll find triple-power nuttiness, with peanut butter,
peanut butter chips, and pecans all in one great cookie.

Joan Whitson Wallace   Severn, Maryland

2 cups flour

2 teaspoons baking soda

½ cup butter or margarine

1 cup granulated sugar

1 cup brown sugar, firmly packed

2 eggs

1 teaspoon vanilla extract

1 cup chunky peanut butter

½ cup chopped pecans

6 ounces (1 cup) semi-sweet chocolate chips

6 ounces (1 cup) peanut butter chips

1. Preheat the oven to 350°F.

2. Sift the flour before measuring, then sift again with the baking soda; set aside.

3. With an electric mixer, in a large bowl, cream together the butter or margarine and sugars. Beat in the eggs and vanilla. Add the peanut butter and beat until well mixed.

4. Stir in the sifted ingredients. Add the pecans, chocolate chips, and peanut butter chips.

5. Drop by teaspoonfuls onto greased baking sheets, spacing about 2 inches apart. Bake for about 12 minutes, or until golden.

Yield: 4 ½ dozen

Hazelnut Butter Chocolate Chip Cookies

*This cookie originated in Oregon's hazelnut country
(in some parts of the United States, hazelnuts are called filberts),
where the availability of hazelnut butter offers a rich
and unusual alternative to peanut butter.*

Verna Kastner 🍫 *Hillsboro, Oregon*

1½ cups flour

¾ teaspoon baking soda

½ teaspoon baking powder

¼ teaspoon salt

½ cup butter or margarine

1 cup crunchy hazelnut butter or peanut butter

½ cup granulated sugar

½ cup brown sugar, firmly packed

½ teaspoon vanilla extract

1 egg

12 ounces (2 cups) semi-sweet chocolate chips

1. Sift together the flour, baking soda, baking powder, and salt; set aside.

2. In a large mixing bowl, cream the butter or margarine, hazelnut or peanut butter, and sugars until the mixture is very light and fluffy. Beat in the vanilla and egg. Stir in the sifted ingredients and mix well. Stir in the chocolate chips.

3. Chill for 2 hours.

4. Preheat the oven to 375°F.

5. Drop by tablespoonfuls onto baking sheets, spacing well apart. Bake for 10 to 12 minutes, or until golden.

Yield: about 3 dozen

AND
They're Good for You, Too

Snacks, even spectacularly good-tasting ones, needn't be empty calories. Most families devour a batch of freshly baked chocolate chip cookies pretty quickly, so why not lace them with wholesome ingredients that not only will take the edge off afterschool and afterwork appetites but also will provide a healthy dose of things that are good for the body: nuts and nut butters, rolled oats and other whole grains, wheat germ and bran, dried fruits, yogurt, honey, and even such improbable ingredients as pinto beans and zucchini.

Sunny Chocolate Chip Cookies

*Sunfower and sesame seeds add not only a nutty,
sweet flavor, but also iron and protein.*

Marilyn Taylor   Winfield, Kansas

1¼ cups all-purpose flour

1 cup whole-wheat flour

1 teaspoon baking soda

½ teaspoon baking powder

¼ teaspoon salt

1 cup butter or margarine, softened

¾ cup granulated sugar

¾ cup brown sugar, firmly packed

2 eggs

1 teaspoon vanilla extract

12 ounces (2 cups) semi-sweet chocolate chips

½ cup salted sunflower kernels

¼ cup sesame seeds

1. Preheat the oven to 375°F.

2. Combine the flours, baking soda, baking powder, and salt; set aside.

3. In a large mixing bowl, cream the butter or margarine. Gradually add the sugars, beating until the mixture is light and fluffy. Add the eggs and vanilla and beat well. Add the dry ingredients to the creamed mixture and beat well. Stir in the chocolate chips, sunflower kernels, and sesame seeds.

4. Drop the dough by heaping teaspoonfuls onto lightly greased baking sheets, spacing well apart. Bake for 8 to 10 minutes, or until golden brown. Cool slightly on baking sheets before removing to wire racks.

Yield: 5 dozen

Whole-Grain and Honey Chocolate Chip Cookies

A somewhat dense cookie, this gets its nutritional value from the combination of whole wheat flour, milk, and nuts.

Diana K. Stava 🍪 Newberg, Oregon

2¼ cups whole-wheat flour

1 teaspoon baking soda

1 teaspoon salt

1 cup butter, margarine, or shortening, softened

⅔ cup honey

¼ cup powdered milk

1 teaspoon vanilla extract

2 eggs

12 ounces (2 cups) semi-sweet chocolate morsels

½–1 cup walnuts, finely chopped

1. Preheat the oven to 375°F.

2. Sift together the flour, baking soda, and salt; set aside.

3. In a large mixing bowl, beat the butter, honey, powdered milk, and vanilla until creamy. Add the eggs. Add the sifted ingredients and blend well. Stir in the chocolate chips and walnuts.

4. Drop by small teaspoonfuls onto lightly greased baking sheets, spacing well apart. Bake for 10 to 12 minutes, or until cookies are just lightly browned.

Yield: about 3 dozen

Chocolate Chip Cookies with Bran

The addition of bran to the traditional chocolate chip cookie recipe makes a pleasant textural change and adds healthful fiber to this dessert or snack.

Marilyn Taylor 🍫 *Winfield, Kansas*

1¼ cups flour

1 teaspoon baking soda

1 teaspoon salt

1 cup unsalted (sweet) butter, at room temperature

¾ cup granulated sugar

¾ cup light brown sugar, firmly packed

1 teaspoon vanilla extract

2 eggs

12 ounces (2 cups) semi-sweet chocolate chips

½ cup finely chopped pecans

½ cup bran

1. Preheat the oven to 350°F.

2. Sift the flour before measuring, then sift again with the baking soda and salt; set aside.

3. In a large mixing bowl, cream together the butter, sugars, and vanilla until smooth. Add the eggs. Stir in the sifted ingredients and mix until well blended. Gently stir in the chocolate chips, pecans, and bran.

4. Form the dough into balls the size of large walnuts. Place on lightly greased baking sheets, allowing room between cookies for expansion. Press down on the balls with lightly water-moistened fingers to flatten. Bake for 10 to 12 minutes, or until golden brown.

Yield: 3 dozen

Nutrilicious
Triple Chocolate Chip Cookies

*Having grown up on a large wheat farm
in Saskatchewan, Canada, Adele appreciates the magic
that wholesome, fresh ingredients bring to any recipe.*

Adele A. Chatfield 🍫 *Portland, Oregon*

1 cup old-fashioned
   rolled oats

1¾ cups flour

1 teaspoon baking soda

⅛ teaspoon salt

½ cup wheat germ

½ cup coconut

1 cup butter, softened

1½ cups brown sugar, firmly
   packed

1½ teaspoons vanilla extract

2 large eggs

12 ounces (2 cups) semi-
   sweet chocolate chips

1 cup chopped walnuts

1. Preheat the oven to 375°F.

2. Place the rolled oats in a blender and whirl at low speed for about 15 seconds. Combine the rolled oats, flour, baking soda, salt, wheat germ, and coconut; set aside.

3. In a large mixing bowl, cream together the butter, sugar, and vanilla until smooth. Beat in the eggs. Gradually add the dry ingredients to the creamed mixture and combine well. Stir in the chocolate chips and nuts.

4. Drop the batter by well-rounded teaspoonfuls onto ungreased baking sheets, spacing well apart. Bake for 10 to 12 minutes, or until golden brown.

Yield: 6½ dozen

Whole-Grain Chocolate Chip Cookies

This hearty cookie recipe originated in Germany many years ago.
For best results, use a real Irish oatmeal, such as
McCann's Quick-Cooking Irish Oatmeal.

Sheila Nusbaum 🍫 *Richmond, Virginia*

1 cup unbleached, all-purpose flour

1 cup stone-ground, whole-wheat flour

1 teaspoon baking soda

½ teaspoon baking powder

Pinch of salt

1 cup granulated sugar

1 cup light brown sugar

1 cup butter (or ½ cup butter and ½ cup margarine, or 1 cup shortening)

2 eggs

1 teaspoon vanilla extract

2 cups quick-cooking rolled oats

12 ounces (2 cups) semi-sweet chocolate chips

1. Preheat the oven to 375°F.

2. Sift together the flours, baking soda, baking powder, and salt; set aside.

3. In a large mixing bowl, cream together the sugars and butter. Add the eggs. Add the sifted ingredients to the creamed mixture. Stir in the vanilla, rolled oats, and chocolate chips.

4. Drop by teaspoonfuls onto lightly greased baking sheets, spacing well apart. Bake for 8 to 10 minutes, or until golden brown. Allow cookies to cool slightly on trays before removing to racks to cool completely.

Yield: about 5 dozen

Carole E.'s Oatmeal Chocolate Chip Cookies

Melting the butter before you add it to the other ingredients causes the cookies to spread more while they bake.

Carole Evans 🍪 Burien, Washington

½ cup rolled oats

2 cups flour

1 teaspoon baking soda

1 cup butter, melted and cooled slightly

¾ cup granulated sugar

¾ cup brown sugar, firmly packed

2 eggs

1 teaspoon vanilla extract

6 ounces (1 cup) semi-sweet chocolate chips

1 cup chopped walnuts

1. Preheat a convection oven to 350°F; preheat a regular oven to 375°F.

2. Place the rolled oats in a blender and grind until fine. Measure out ¼ cup and sift it together with the flour and the baking soda. Set aside.

3. In a large mixing bowl, combine the melted butter, sugars, and eggs; blend until smooth. Stir in the vanilla. Stir in the sifted ingredients and mix well. Add the chocolate chips and walnuts.

4. Drop by rounded tablespoonfuls onto greased baking sheets, spacing well apart. Bake in a convection oven for 10 to 12 minutes; in a regular oven, for about 10 minutes.

Yield: about 3 dozen

Carol C.'s Oatmeal Chocolate Chip Cookies

Shortening and extra egg yolks make a soft, chewy cookie.

Carol Campbell  *Midwest City, Oklahoma*

2¼ cups flour

1 teaspoon baking soda

1 teaspoon salt

½ cup butter, softened

½ cup shortening

¾ cup granulated sugar

¾ cup brown sugar, firmly packed

1 teaspoon vanilla extract

1 whole egg

2 egg yolks

¼ cup rolled oats

12 ounces (2 cups) semi-sweet chocolate chips

1 cup nuts, chopped

1. Preheat the oven to 375°F.

2. Combine the flour, baking soda, and salt; set aside.

3. In a large bowl, combine the butter, shortening, sugars, and vanilla, and cream until fluffy. Add the egg and the egg yolks; beat well.

4. Gradually add all but about ½ cup of the dry ingredients. Mix the rolled oats with the remaining flour mixture and stir into the batter. Stir in the chocolate chips and nuts.

5. Drop by heaping teaspoonfuls onto ungreased baking sheets, spacing well apart. Bake for 10 to 12 minutes, or until golden brown.

Yield: about 5 dozen

Irene's Oatmeal Chocolate Chip Cookies

This old family recipe has been updated over the years — first with raisins, then with chocolate chips. It comes from a tradition in which the cookie jar is the symbol of hospitality and cookies are the reward for almost everything.

Irene G. Carter ✿ *El Paso, Texas*

1 cup quick-cooking rolled oats

⅓ cup flour

1 teaspoon baking powder

¼ teaspoon salt

½ cup sugar

1 egg, well beaten

1 tablespoon corn oil

1 teaspoon vanilla extract

½ cup shredded coconut

6 ounces (1 cup) semi-sweet chocolate chips

½ cup chopped nuts

1. Preheat the oven to 350°F.

2. In a large mixing bowl, stir together the rolled oats, flour, baking powder, salt, and sugar. Mix in the beaten egg. Add the corn oil and vanilla and blend well. Stir in the coconut, chocolate chips, and nuts and mix well.

3. Drop by teaspoonfuls onto lightly oiled baking sheets, spacing cookies about 2 inches apart. Bake for 8 to 10 minutes, or until golden brown. Remove from baking trays to cooling racks while still hot.

Yield: about 3 dozen

Once-around-the-Kitchen Cookies

Do too many flavors spoil the cookie? Not in this case! Peanut butter, oats, walnuts, raisins, coconut, and, of course, chocolate marry happily in this lively mix.

Sandy Paulsrud ❧ *Nielsville, Minnesota*

2 cups flour

1 teaspoon baking soda

1 cup butter

½ cup peanut butter

1 cup brown sugar, firmly packed

½ cup granulated sugar

2 eggs

1½ cups rolled oats

½ cup chopped walnuts

½ cup raisins

12 ounces (2 cups) semi-sweet chocolate chips

½ cup flaked coconut

1. Preheat the oven to 375°F.

2. Combine the flour and baking soda; set aside.

3. In a large mixing bowl, cream the butter, peanut butter, and sugars. Beat in the eggs. Add the rolled oats, walnuts, raisins, chocolate chips, and coconut. Add the dry ingredients and mix thoroughly.

4. Drop dough by teaspoonfuls onto ungreased baking sheets, spacing well apart. Bake for about 10 minutes, or until golden brown.

Yield: about 4 dozen

Cowgirl Cookies

Copious amounts of shortening and egg give these cookies a shortbread-like texture.

Bev Almaguer and Nancy Fry 🍫 *Fargo, North Dakota*

4 cups flour

2 teaspoons baking soda

1 teaspoon baking powder

1 teaspoon salt

2 cups shortening

2 cups granulated sugar

2 cups brown sugar, firmly packed

4 eggs

3 cups quick-cooking rolled oats

2 teaspoons vanilla extract

12 ounces (2 cups) semi-sweet chocolate chips

1. Preheat the oven to 350°F.

2. Sift together the flour, baking soda, baking powder, and salt; set aside.

3. In a large mixing bowl, combine the shortening and sugars, then cream well. Beat in the eggs until they are thoroughly blended. Stir in the dry ingredients and mix well. Add the rolled oats, vanilla, and chocolate chips.

4. Drop by teaspoonfuls onto greased baking sheets, spacing well apart. Bake for about 12 minutes, or until cookies are golden brown.

Yield: 8 to 9 dozen

Oatmeal and Milk Chocolate Chunk Cookies

*Although these cookies may not appear done at the
end of baking time, they are. They're meant to be soft cookies,
and overbaking will ruin them.*

Edry Naddour Goot 🍪 Phoenix, Arizona

2 cups flour

1 teaspoon baking powder

1 teaspoon baking soda

2½ cups rolled oats

1 cup unsalted (sweet) butter, softened

1 cup granulated sugar

1 cup brown sugar, firmly packed

2 eggs

1 teaspoon vanilla extract

12 ounces (2 cups) semi-sweet chocolate chips

1 (8-ounce) milk chocolate bar, grated

1½ cups chopped nuts

1. Preheat the oven to 400°F.

2. Sift together the flour, baking powder, and baking soda; set aside.

3. Whirl the rolled oats in a food processor or blender until they are reduced to a fine powder. Mix into the other dry ingredients and set aside.

4. In a large mixing bowl, cream the butter and sugars. Blend in the eggs until the mixture is smooth and creamy. Stir in the vanilla. Gradually add the sifted ingredients to the creamed mixture, stirring well after each addition; the batter will be stiff. Mix in the chocolate chips, grated chocolate, and nuts.

5. Place golf ball–sized pieces of dough about 2 inches apart on ungreased baking sheets. Do not flatten dough. Bake for about 8 minutes. Cookies will appear underdone. *Do not overbake.*

Yield: 3 dozen

Gramma's Choc-o-Chips

I wish my grandmother had had a copy of this recipe when I was growing up! The combination of margarine and shortening makes the kind of "short" cookie I like, and the two kinds of chocolate will satisfy any sweet tooth.

Catherine Rivers   Dalton, Massachusetts

½ cup margarine

½ cup shortening

1 cup granulated sugar

½ cup brown sugar

1 teaspoon salt

1 teaspoon baking soda

2 eggs

1 teaspoon vanilla extract

2 cups quick-cooking rolled oats

1⅓ cups all-purpose flour (or more to make a stiff dough)

1 cup semisweet chocolate chips

1 cup chocolate chunks or large chips

1. Preheat the oven to 375°F.

2. In a large mixing bowl, combine thoroughly the margarine, shortening, sugars, salt, baking soda, eggs, and vanilla. Add the oats and flour. (You should have a very stiff dough.) Add the chocolate chips and chunks.

3. Drop by teaspoonfuls onto ungreased baking sheets, spacing well apart. Bake for 8 to 10 minutes, or until golden brown.

Yield: about 5 dozen

Choco-O's

*Try adding raisins or, for a more festive treat at Christmas,
some chopped candied fruit to this cookie dough.*

Jesse B. Pyle   Marine City, Mississippi

2 cups flour

1 teaspoon baking soda

2 cups quick-cooking
  rolled oats

1 cup butter or margarine

1 cup granulated sugar

1 cup brown sugar, packed

2 eggs

1 teaspoon vanilla extract

½ teaspoon almond extract

1 cup chopped nuts

12 ounces (2 cups) semi-
  sweet chocolate chips

1. Preheat the oven to 375°F.

2. Sift together the flour and baking soda. Add the oats and set aside.

3. In a large mixing bowl, cream the butter or margarine and sugars. Add the eggs one at a time, beating after each addition, until the mixture is creamy. Fold in the sifted ingredients. Stir in the vanilla and almond extracts. Gently mix in the nuts and chocolate chips.

4. Drop by teaspoonfuls onto greased baking sheets, spacing cookies 2 inches apart. Bake for 10 to 12 minutes, or until cookies are lightly browned.

Yield: 5 dozen

Oatmeal and Sour Cream Chocolate Chip Cookies

*This rich cookie is made with rolled oats and sour cream
for added texture and flavor.*

Marianne McBride 🍫 *Pacifica, California*

2 cups flour

1 teaspoon baking soda

½ teaspoon salt

1 cup rolled oats

1¼ cups light brown sugar, firmly packed

1 cup unsalted (sweet) butter or margarine

2 eggs

1 teaspoon vanilla extract

½ cup sour cream

12 ounces (2 cups) semi-sweet chocolate chips

12 ounces (2 cups) milk chocolate morsels

¼ cup raisins

¾ cup walnuts, coarsely chopped

¾ cup pecans, coarsely chopped

1. Preheat the oven to 350°F.

2. Sift together the flour, baking soda, and salt. Stir in the rolled oats and set aside.

3. In a large bowl, cream together the sugar and butter or margarine until the mixture is light and fluffy. Beat in the eggs and vanilla. Add the sifted ingredients to the creamed mixture until just blended. Add the sour cream and mix until just blended. Stir in the chocolates, raisins, and nuts.

4. Drop dough by heaping teaspoonfuls onto ungreased baking sheets, spacing cookies 2 inches apart. Bake for 12 to 15 minutes, or until cookies are lightly browned around the edges. Allow to cool on baking trays for 5 minutes before removing to racks to cool completely.

Yield: about 5½ dozen

Peanut Butter and Oatmeal Chocolate Chip Cookies

Use a light touch while working with this dough:
Do not overbeat and do not overbake.

Lovell McGillicuddy 🍫 *Cedar Rapids, Iowa*

3 cups flour

3 teaspoons baking soda

1½ teaspoons salt

1½ cups quick-cooking rolled oats

1½ cups granulated sugar

1½ cups brown sugar

1½ cups margarine

1½ cups peanut butter

1½ teaspoons vanilla extract

3 eggs

12 ounces (2 cups) semi-sweet chocolate chips

1 cup chopped nuts

1. Sift together the flour, baking soda, and salt. Stir in the rolled oats and set aside.

2. In a large bowl, cream together the sugars, margarine, and peanut butter. Add the vanilla and eggs, then beat well. Add the sifted ingredients and mix well. Add the chocolate chips and nuts. Chill for 2 hours.

3. Preheat the oven to 375°F.

4. Form the dough into walnut-sized balls and place on ungreased baking sheets, spacing well apart. Bake for 10 to 15 minutes, or until golden. Do not overbake.

Yield: 5 to 6 dozen

Molasses and Oatmeal Chocolate Chip Cookies

A favorite family recipe features the old-fashioned taste of molasses and spices.

Harriet A. Kemp   Seattle, Washington

1½ cups flour

1 teaspoon baking soda

½ teaspoon ground cloves

½ teaspoon ginger

½ teaspoon salt

1 cup sugar

¾ cup butter

1 egg

¼ cup dark molasses

¾ cup quick-cooking rolled oats

½ cup raisins

6 ounces (1 cup) semi-sweet chocolate chips

1. Preheat the oven to 375°F.

2. Sift the flour before measuring, then sift again with the baking soda, cloves, ginger, salt, and sugar; set aside.

3. In a large mixing bowl, cream the butter and egg. Add the sifted ingredients and beat with an electric mixer until the batter is smooth, about 2 minutes.

4. Blend in the molasses, rolled oats, raisins, and chocolate chips. The dough will be quite sticky.

5. Drop by rounded tablespoonfuls onto ungreased baking sheets, spacing well apart. Bake for 8 to 10 minutes, or until golden brown. Cool before removing from baking sheets.

Yield: 2 dozen

Granola Chocolate Chip Cookies

*This rather hard, crisp, granola-like cookie stores well in
airtight canisters or zipper-lock bags.*

D. Michael Pitalo 🍪 Baton Rouge, Louisiana

2 cups flour

2 teaspoons baking soda

1 teaspoon baking powder

½ teaspoon salt

1 cup shortening

1 cup granulated sugar

1 cup light brown sugar,
firmly packed

1 teaspoon vanilla extract

2 eggs

2 cups rolled oats

2 cups corn flakes

1 cup shredded coconut

1 cup salted peanuts

6 ounces (1 cup) semi-
sweet chocolate chips

1. Preheat the oven to 350°F.

2. Sift together the flour, baking soda, baking powder,
and salt; set aside.

3. In a large mixing bowl, beat together the shortening,
sugars, and vanilla until light and creamy. Add the
eggs one at a time, mixing thoroughly after each
addition. Blend until the mixture is uniform in color.

4. Add the sifted ingredients, one-half cup at a time,
mixing thoroughly after each addition. Add the
rolled oats, corn flakes, coconut, nuts, and chocolate
chips. Mix with your hands, as the dough will be stiff
and dry. Knead well to ensure thorough blending,
then shape the mixture into a tight ball.

5. Pinch off 2-inch balls and roll them tightly. Place
cookies on ungreased baking sheets, spacing well
apart, and press into button shapes. Cook only as
many sheets at one time as will allow good air circulation in the oven. Bake for 12 to 15 minutes or until
cookies are golden brown. Cool on sheets for 2 or
3 minutes; remove to wire racks to finish cooling.

Yield: about 6 dozen

Pacific Pride
Chocolate Chip Cookies

Created by an anthropologist who enjoys seeing the connection between food and where it is grown, this recipe is named for the sources of its ingredients: Hawaiian sugars, Washington State wheats, South Pacific coconuts, and Oregon hazelnuts.

Shirley Ewart 🍪 *Tigard, Oregon*

1 cup hazelnuts, chopped

2 cups flour

1 cup margarine

1 cup granulated sugar

1 cup brown sugar

2 eggs

1 teaspoon vanilla extract

1 teaspoon baking soda

½ teaspoon baking powder

¼ teaspoon salt

2 cups rolled oats

1 cup bran, corn, or wheat flakes

1 cup coconut

1 generous cup milk chocolate chips

1. Spread the nuts on a baking sheet and toast them lightly in a 350°F oven. Set them aside to cool.

2. Preheat the oven to 300°F.

3. Sift the flour and set it aside.

4. In a very large bowl, cream the margarine, sugars, and eggs. Add the vanilla, baking soda, baking powder, and salt. Add the flour and mix well.

5. Stir in the rolled oats, bran flakes, coconut, toasted and cooled hazelnuts, and chocolate chips. Mix well.

6. Drop by teaspoonfuls onto greased baking sheets, spacing well apart. Bake for 12 minutes.

Yield: about 7 dozen

Nutritious Chocolate Chip Cookies

*Try different combinations of the suggested optional ingredients
for a great-tasting — and good-for-you — cookie every time.*

Donna Smyrk   Rochester, Minnesota

2¼ cups flour, divided

2 cups brown sugar, firmly
packed

1 teaspoon baking soda

1 cup butter or margarine,
softened

2 teaspoons vanilla extract

2 eggs

2 cups rolled oats

12 ounces (2 cups) semi-
sweet chocolate chips

½ cup nuts or sunflower
seeds

Optional Ingredients
(use one or more of the following):

1 cup peanut butter

1 cup wheat germ

1 cup flaked coconut

1 cup dry milk

1. Preheat the oven to 350°F.

2. Combine 1¼ cups of the flour and the brown sugar,
baking soda, butter or margarine, vanilla, and eggs,
and beat with an electric mixer at medium speed until
well blended. Stir in the rolled oats, chocolate chips,
nuts, and any of the optional ingredients by hand.

3. Drop dough by rounded teaspoonfuls onto ungreased
cookie sheets, spacing cookies about 2 inches apart.
Bake for 10 minutes.

Yield: 6 to 7 dozen

Mocha Pinto Chippers

Vary this recipe by substituting chopped dates or chopped golden raisins for the apricots. The cookies will still be moist and chewy.

Margaret Rhodes 🍃 Prescott, Arizona

1 can (16 ounces) pinto beans, well drained

2 cups flour

1 teaspoon baking soda

½ teaspoon salt

1½ teaspoons instant coffee granules

3 tablespoons unsweetened cocoa

1 cup quick-cooking rolled oats

½ cup plus 2 teaspoons unsalted (sweet) butter, divided

½ cup shortening

1 cup brown sugar, firmly packed

¾ cup granulated sugar

¼ cup honey

1 egg

1 teaspoon vanilla extract

15 ounces (2½ cups) semi-sweet chocolate chips

½ cup chopped dried apricots

1. Preheat the oven to 350°F.

2. Purée the drained pinto beans in a blender, in a food processor, or with a ricer. Measure 1 cup and set aside.

3. In a large bowl, combine the flour, baking soda, salt, coffee granules, cocoa, and oats. Set aside.

4. In another large mixing bowl, cream together ½ cup of the butter and the shortening. Gradually add the sugars and honey, beating until the mixture is fluffy. Add the egg, vanilla, and 1 cup of bean puree. Mix to blend thoroughly. Stir in the dry ingredients, then mix until completely blended. Gently stir in 1½ cups of the chocolate chips and the chopped apricots.

5. Drop by tablespoonfuls onto lightly greased baking sheets, spacing well apart. Flatten each cookie slightly with the back of a spoon. Bake for 15 to 18 minutes, or until golden brown. Bake longer for firmer, crisper cookies. Remove to wire racks to cool.

6. In a saucepan, melt together the remaining chocolate chips and the rest of the butter. Drizzle across the cookies in a zigzag pattern. Allow the chocolate to set before storing the cookies.

Yield: 5 dozen

Zesty Zucchini Chocolate Chip Cookies

Have you ever dreamed of adding zucchini to your chocolate chip cookies? The combination tastes better than it sounds! Rich in spices and chocolate, these cookies are sure to please.

Christine E. Shamanoff 🍪 Fort Wayne, Indiana

1¼ cups all-purpose flour

1¼ cups whole-wheat flour

2 teaspoons baking powder

¼ teaspoon baking soda

¼ teaspoon salt

1 teaspoon cinnamon

½ teaspoon nutmeg

½ teaspoon ginger

½ teaspoon ground cloves

¼ cup unsalted (sweet) butter, softened

1 cup light brown sugar, firmly packed

½ cup granulated sugar

1 egg

1 teaspoon orange extract

1½ cups grated zucchini

1 cup chopped walnuts

6 ounces (1 cup) semi-sweet chocolate chips

1. Preheat the oven to 350°F.

2. Sift together the flours, baking powder, baking soda, salt, cinnamon, nutmeg, ginger, and cloves. Set aside.

3. In a large mixing bowl, beat the butter and sugars until the mixture is light and fluffy. Beat in the egg and the orange extract. Add the grated zucchini and mix well. Add the dry sifted ingredients, stirring until they are well blended. Gently fold in the walnuts and chocolate chips.

4. Drop by tablespoonfuls onto greased baking sheets, spacing cookies well apart. Bake for about 12 minutes, or until cookies are lightly brown.

Yield: 6½ dozen

DOUBLE
Chocolate Chip Cookies

We now enter the realm of the serious chocolate eaters — those who believe that if *some* chocolate is good, *twice* as much is better. These gourmets find chocolate chips alone inadequate to satisfy their longings; they desire their chocolate chips surrounded by a rich chocolate cookie.

Prize-Winning Double Chocolate Chip Cookies

Grand Prize

The grand prize winner of all 2,600 submitted to The Orchards' 1987 contest is this rich, moist, double-chocolate cookie.

Junior League of Las Vegas ❧ Las Vegas, Nevada

This recipe was first published in Winning at the Table, *by the Junior League of Las Vegas.*

1¾ cups flour

¼ teaspoon baking soda

1 cup butter or margarine, softened

1 teaspoon vanilla extract

1 cup granulated sugar

½ cup dark brown sugar, firmly packed

1 egg

⅓ cup unsweetened cocoa

2 tablespoons milk

1 cup chopped pecans or walnuts

6 ounces (1 cup) semi-sweet chocolate chips

1. Preheat the oven to 350°F.

2. Combine the flour and baking soda; set aside.

3. Using an electric mixer, in a large bowl, cream the butter or margarine. Add the vanilla and sugars, then beat until fluffy. Beat in the egg. At low speed, beat in the cocoa, then the milk. With a wooden spoon, mix in the dry ingredients just until blended. Stir in the nuts and chocolate chips.

4. Drop by rounded teaspoonfuls onto nonstick or foil-lined baking sheets, spacing well apart. Bake for 12 to 13 minutes. Remove from the oven and cool slightly before transferring to a cooling rack.

Yield: 3 dozen

Catherine's Double Chocolate Chip Cookies

*These mouthwatering cookies are soft and chewy,
and likely to stay that way — if you can keep them around.*

Catherine C. Thomas 🍪 Columbus, Ohio

3 cups flour

1 cup plus 2 tablespoons
unsweetened cocoa

1½ teaspoons baking soda

¾ teaspoon salt

1¾ cups plus 2 tablespoons
butter or margarine

3 cups sugar

3 eggs

1 teaspoon vanilla extract

12 ounces (2 cups) semi-
sweet chocolate chips

1½ cups chopped pecans
(optional)

1. Preheat the oven to 350°F.

2. Combine the flour, cocoa, baking soda, and salt;
set aside.

3. In a large mixing bowl, cream the butter or margarine
and sugar until the mixture is light and fluffy. Add
the eggs and vanilla, then beat well. Blend the dry
ingredients into the creamed mixture. Stir in the
chocolate chips and nuts.

4. Drop tablespoonfuls of the dough onto ungreased
baking sheets, spacing well apart. Bake for 8 or 9
minutes — cookies will still be soft. Cool slightly on
the baking sheets before removing cookies to cooling
racks. Store in an airtight container.

Yield: 6 dozen

Marjorie's Double Chocolate Chip Cookies

Conceived by combining a brownie recipe with a chocolate chip cookie recipe, this is a creation for the chocolate fanatics among us — deep, rich chocolate through and through. Watch carefully while baking; these cookies burn easily.

Marjorie Gross   Green Bay, Wisconsin

2¼ cups flour

¾ cup unsweetened cocoa

1 teaspoon baking soda

½ teaspoon salt

1¼ cups margarine

1½ cups sugar

2 tablespoons corn syrup

2 eggs

2 teaspoons vanilla extract

1 cup chopped nuts

12 ounces (2 cups) semi-sweet chocolate chips

1. Preheat the oven to 350°F.

2. Combine the flour, cocoa, baking soda, and salt; set aside.

3. In a large mixing bowl, cream the margarine and sugar. Add the corn syrup, eggs, and vanilla, then blend well. Gradually blend the dry ingredients into the creamed mixture. Stir in the nuts and the chocolate chips.

4. Drop by teaspoonfuls onto ungreased baking sheets, spacing well apart. Bake for about 10 minutes. Do not overbake. Cookies will be soft and puffy when you take them out, but they will flatten when cool.

Yield: 4½ dozen

Dorothy's Double Chocolate Chip Cookies

A soft, flavorful cookie, this double chocolate chip cookie will delight the most discerning palate.

Dorothy Lent   Columbus, Ohio

2 cups flour

¼ cup unsweetened cocoa

½ teaspoon salt

1 cup margarine, at room temperature

¾ cup granulated sugar

¾ cup brown sugar, firmly packed

2 eggs

1 teaspoon vanilla extract

1 teaspoon baking soda

1 tablespoon hot water

12 ounces (2 cups) semi-sweet chocolate chips

2 cups chopped walnuts

1. Preheat the oven to 350°F.

2. Mix the flour, cocoa, and salt; set aside.

3. In a large mixing bowl, cream the margarine until it is smooth, then add the sugars. Add the eggs and vanilla, then beat until the mixture is pale and fluffy. Stir in *half* of the dry ingredients.

4. In another large bowl, stir the baking soda into the water. Add this to the batter, then stir in the remaining flour until the mixture is well blended. Gently stir in the chocolate chips and nuts.

5. Drop by heaping teaspoonfuls onto greased baking sheets (or baking sheets covered with ungreased pieces of foil), spacing cookies about 2 inches apart. Bake 10 to 12 minutes, or until cookies appear firm.

Yield: 3½ to 4 dozen

Gloria's Double Chocolate Chip Cookies

Perfect for true chocolate lovers, these cookies are unforgettable.

Gloria MacDonald  *Chadds Ford, Pennsylvania*

1¾ cups flour

¼ cup cocoa

1 teaspoon baking soda

½ teaspoon salt

¾ cup brown sugar, firmly packed

½ cup granulated sugar

1 cup butter, softened

1 teaspoon vanilla extract

1 egg

6 ounces (1 cup) semi-sweet chocolate chips

½ cup chopped nuts (optional)

1. Preheat the oven to 375°F.

2. Sift together the flour, cocoa, baking soda, and salt; set aside.

3. In a large mixing bowl, cream together the sugars and butter until the mixture is light and fluffy. Blend in the vanilla and egg. Add the sifted ingredients to the creamed mixture. Gently stir in the chocolate chips and nuts.

4. Drop by teaspoonfuls onto ungreased baking sheets, spacing well apart. Bake for 7 to 11 minutes, or until the dough is set. Do not overbake. Let cool 1 minute before transferring cookies to a cooling rack.

Yield: 3 dozen

Brownie Chocolate Chips

These cookies are a serendipitous combination of those two all-time favorites: brownies and chocolate chip cookies. This recipe is also delicious when made with macadamia nuts or walnuts instead of pecans, and with mint-chocolate chips, peanut butter chips, or butterscotch chips instead of semisweet chocolate chips. Or try substituting 1 teaspoon of mint flavoring for one of the teaspoons of vanilla.

Victoria Baxter 🍪 Birmingham, Alabama

1⅓ cups flour

1 teaspoon baking powder

½ teaspoon salt

1 cup butter

4 squares (1-ounce) unsweetened chocolate

4 eggs

2 cups granulated sugar

2 teaspoons vanilla extract

6 ounces (1 cup) semisweet chocolate chips

½ cup chopped pecans

1. Preheat the oven to 350°F.

2. Sift together the flour, baking powder, and salt; set aside.

3. In a double boiler, melt the butter and chocolate squares; cool slightly.

4. With an electric mixer, beat the eggs until they are well blended. Gradually add the sugar and vanilla. Stir in the chocolate mixture by hand. Stir in the dry ingredients and gently add the chocolate chips.

5. Pour into a greased 9- x 13- x 2-inch pan. Sprinkle the nuts over the top. Bake for 30 minutes. Cut while still warm. Store in the refrigerator.

Yield: about 24 bars

Fudge Fantasies

Simple but elegant, and sure to satisfy that chocolate craving.

Celia A. Keel 🍫 *Hutchinson, Kansas*

1½ cups flour

½ teaspoon baking soda

¼ teaspoon salt

¼ cup unsweetened cocoa

½ cup butter

1¼ cups brown sugar, firmly packed

2 eggs

1 teaspoon vanilla extract

⅓ cup pecans, chopped

½ cup semisweet chocolate minichips

1. Sift together the flour, baking soda, salt, and cocoa; set aside.

2. In a large mixing bowl, cream together the butter and the sugar until the mixture is light. Add the eggs one at a time, beating well after each addition. Add the vanilla. Fold the sifted ingredients into the creamed mixture. Stir in the nuts and chocolate chips.

3. Chill the dough for 1 hour.

4. Preheat the oven to 350°F.

5. Drop the dough by teaspoonfuls onto greased baking sheets, spacing well apart. Bake for 10 minutes. Cool slightly, but remove cookies from baking trays while they are still warm.

Yield: about 3 dozen

Brown-and-White Chocolate Chip Cookies

White chocolate may not qualify as
"real" chocolate, but who'll complain?
Especially with this recipe's added kick of cocoa.

Frances C. Fulwider 🍫 *Carmel, New York*

1 cup flour

½ teaspoon baking powder

½ teaspoon salt

3 tablespoons unsweet-
ened cocoa

½ cup shortening

¾ cup granulated sugar

1 egg

½ teaspoon vanilla extract

6 ounces (1 cup) white
chocolate, broken into
small bits

½ cup chopped nuts

1. Preheat the oven to 375°F.

2. Mix together the flour, baking powder, salt, and
cocoa; set aside.

3. In a large mixing bowl, cream together the shortening and sugar. Add the egg and vanilla, then beat
until the mixture is fluffy. Gradually add the dry
ingredients, mixing well. Add the chocolate bits
and nuts.

4. Drop by teaspoonfuls onto ungreased baking sheets,
spacing well apart. Bake for 10 minutes.

Yield: 2½ to 3 dozen

Ice Cream Chocolate Chip Cookies

Chocolate ice cream and unsweetened cocoa give this cookie a moist, fudgelike taste. To ensure a moist cookie, be careful not to overbake. Note: These cookies don't freeze well.

Gloria Dutrumble ✿ *Uncasville, Connecticut*

1¼ cups flour

½ teaspoon baking soda

½ teaspoon salt

¾ cup margarine, softened

½ cup granulated sugar

½ cup light brown sugar, firmly packed

⅓ cup unsweetened cocoa

1½ teaspoons vanilla extract

1 large egg

⅓ cup chocolate ice cream, softened

6 ounces (1 cup) semi-sweet chocolate chips

¾ cup coarsely chopped walnuts

1. Preheat the oven to 350°F.

2. Combine the flour, baking soda, and salt; set aside.

3. In a large mixing bowl, combine the margarine, sugars, cocoa, and vanilla, then beat until creamy. Add the egg and ice cream; beat well. Gradually add the dry ingredients and mix well. Stir in the chocolate chips and walnuts.

4. Drop by well-rounded teaspoonfuls onto lightly greased baking sheets, spacing cookies about 2 inches apart. Bake for 14 to 16 minutes, or until the cookies are well set. Do not overbake.

Yield: about 4 dozen

Cheesy
Double Chocolate Chip Cookies

Inspired by chocolate cheesecake and created to indulge a love for both cream cheese and chocolate, these cookies taste even better the second day, when the cheese has mellowed and the flavors have blended nicely. For variety, try using mint chocolate or white chocolate chips in place of some or all of the semisweet chocolate chips.

Lynda L. Henderson   Ogden, Utah

3½ cups flour

½ cup unsweetened cocoa

1½ teaspoons baking soda

½ teaspoon salt

1 cup shortening

1 package (8 ounces) cream cheese, softened to room temperature

1 cup granulated sugar

1 cup brown sugar, firmly packed

3 extra-large eggs

2 teaspoons vanilla extract

12 ounces (2 cups) semi-sweet chocolate chips

1 cup pecan pieces

1. Preheat the oven to 350°F.

2. Sift the flour before measuring, then sift again with the cocoa, baking soda, and salt; set aside.

3. In a large mixing bowl, cream together the shortening, cream cheese, and sugars. Add the eggs one at a time, beating well after each addition. Add the vanilla and mix well. Add the sifted ingredients and blend well. Stir in the chocolate chips and nuts.

4. Drop by teaspoonfuls onto baking sheets lined with parchment paper, spacing well apart. Bake for 10 to 12 minutes, or until cookies are well set. Do not overbake.

Yield: about 4 dozen

Mainliners

These are the cookies to bake when you need the most chocolate in a chocolate chip cookie . . . NOW! Though the combination of bittersweet and semisweet chocolate chips is inspired, all semisweet chips will suffice in a real emergency.

Janice Stangland   Cedar Rapids, Iowa

2 ounces unsweetened chocolate

¼ cup butter

¼ cup shortening

½ cup dark brown sugar, firmly packed

⅓ cup granulated sugar

1½ teaspoons vanilla extract

¼ teaspoon salt

2 eggs

½ teaspoon baking soda

½ teaspoon cream of tartar

¼ cup plus 2 tablespoons rolled oats

¾ cup flour

⅔ cup walnuts, coarsely chopped

¾ cup bittersweet chocolate chunks

¾ cup semisweet chocolate chips

1. In a small saucepan, carefully melt the unsweetened chocolate over very low heat. Set aside to cool.

2. In a large mixing bowl, combine the butter, shortening, sugars, vanilla, and salt. Beat until fluffy. Beat in the eggs, baking soda, and cream of tartar. Stir in the cooled chocolate.

3. Place the rolled oats in a blender or food processor and grind into a fine powder. Add this to the batter along with the flour. Stir in the chopped nuts and chocolate chunks and chips.

4. Cover the bowl and refrigerate for at least 4 hours.

5. Preheat the oven to 325°F.

6. Using about 2 tablespoons of dough per cookie, shape the dough into balls. Place cookies on lightly greased baking sheets about 1½ inches apart. Bake for 10 to 12 minutes, or until cookie springs back when you press the center lightly with your finger. Do not overbake. Cool on the sheets for 2 minutes. Transfer to paper towels for another minute, and then to cooling racks.

Yield: 2½ dozen

SPECIAL OCCASION
Chocolate Chip Cookies

The final selection of recipes is for those times when you feel expansive and really want to gild the lily. Many of these cookies are no more difficult to make than any others in this book, but because of their special ingredients, such as imported chocolates or fancy liqueurs, some are more expensive. They also are likely to be extravagant in their supply of calories, with no stinting of chocolate, butter, eggs, and spirits. Have fun! These are the cookies to experiment with when you've got some extra time and have an urge to be more creative in the kitchen.

Chocolate Chip Meringues

With crisp outsides and delicious, chewy insides, these bars are well worth the calories! To maintain crispness, particularly in humid weather, be sure to store them in airtight containers.

Ann Marie McCrystal 🍫 Vero Beach, Florida

2 cups flour

1 teaspoon baking powder

¼ teaspoon baking soda

1 cup butter

1½ cups light brown sugar, firmly packed and divided

½ cup granulated sugar

2 eggs, separated

1 teaspoon vanilla extract

12 ounces (2 cups) semi-sweet chocolate chips

½ cup grated coconut (optional)

1. Preheat the oven to 350°F.

2. Sift together the flour, baking powder, and baking soda; set aside.

3. In a large mixing bowl, cream the butter, ½ cup of the brown sugar, and the granulated sugar. Beat in the egg yolks. Gradually add the dry ingredients, mixing well. Stir in the vanilla.

4. Spread the dough onto a 9- x 15-inch baking sheet. Sprinkle with the chocolate chips and press them into the dough.

5. To make a meringue, beat the egg whites until they are stiff. Gradually add the remaining brown sugar, continuing to beat until well mixed. Spread the meringue over the cookie dough, then sprinkle with the coconut.

6. Bake for 25 minutes. When cool, cut into squares.

Yield: 12 large or 24 small bars

Brownie Chip Meringues

*Chewy chocolate and nuts enveloped
in an airy meringue make a festive treat.*

Margaret A. Lane 🍫 Versailles, Kentucky

15 ounces (2½ cups) semi-
sweet chocolate chips,
divided

 4 egg whites

⅛ teaspoon salt

 1 teaspoon vanilla extract

 1 teaspoon cider vinegar

 1 cup granulated sugar

 1 cup chopped walnuts or
pecans

1. Preheat the oven to 350°F.

2. In a small saucepan, carefully melt 2 cups of the chocolate chips and set aside to cool.

3. Beat the egg whites with the salt, vanilla, and vinegar until the mixture stands in soft peaks. Gradually add the sugar, beating again until stiff peaks form.

4. Fold in the melted chocolate, the remaining chocolate chips, and the nuts.

5. Drop by tablespoons onto greased baking sheets, spacing well apart. Bake for about 10 minutes, or until firm. Do not overbake. Store in airtight cookie tins.

Yield: 6 dozen

Old Vienna Chip Cookies

Poppy seeds, cinnamon, apple, walnuts, currants, and chocolate —
all are chosen to conjure memories of favorite Viennese pastries.

Roxanne E. Chan   *Albany, California*

1¼ cups flour

½ teaspoon baking soda

¼ teaspoon salt

½ cup butter

1 cup granulated sugar

1 egg

½ teaspoon cinnamon

½ teaspoon grated lemon zest

2 tablespoons poppy seeds

¼ cup unpeeled, grated, tart apple

9 ounces (1½ cups) semi-sweet chocolate chips

¼ cup chopped walnuts

¼ cup currants

1. Preheat the oven to 375°F.

2. Sift the flour, baking soda, and salt; set aside.

3. In a large mixing bowl, cream the butter. Gradually add the sugar and beat until the mixture is creamy. Beat in the egg, cinnamon, lemon zest, poppy seeds, and apple. Stir in the sifted ingredients and mix well. Gently stir in the chocolate chips, nuts, and currants.

4. Drop the batter by teaspoonfuls onto greased baking sheets, spacing cookies well apart. Bake for 10 minutes.

Yield: 3 dozen

Apple-Kissed Chocolate Chip Cookies

For special occasions, try dipping cool cookies first into melted semisweet chocolate, then into a mixture of crushed apple-cinnamon chips and ground nuts.

Cherry C. Queen 🍫 San Antonio, Texas

2 cups flour

1 teaspoon baking soda

1 teaspoon salt

½ cup quick-cooking rolled oats

½ teaspoon cinnamon

¼ cup minced dried apples

½ cup butter

½ cup shortening

¾ cup granulated sugar

¾ cup brown sugar, firmly packed

1 egg

1 egg yolk

½ teaspoon vanilla extract

1½ tablespoons apple brandy

1 cup coarsely chopped nuts

6 ounces (1 cup) semisweet chocolate chips

1. Preheat the oven to 350°F.

2. Sift together the flour, baking soda, and salt. Add the oats, cinnamon, and dried apples, then mix thoroughly. Set aside.

3. In a large mixing bowl, cream together the butter, shortening, and sugars. Add the egg, egg yolk, vanilla, and apple brandy, then beat until well blended. Add the sifted ingredients and mix well. Stir in the nuts and chocolate chips until they are well distributed.

4. Drop the dough by large tablespoonfuls onto greased baking sheets, spacing cookies about 3 inches apart. To give cookies a more uniform appearance, flatten them slightly with the bottom of a glass dipped in sugar. Bake for 9 to 12 minutes; use the longer baking time for a crisper cookie. Cool on the baking sheets for 2 or 3 minutes before removing the cookies to cooling racks.

Yield: about 3 dozen

Kentucky Derby Chip Delights

From Kentucky Derby country comes this bourbon-flavored cookie,
rich in brown sugar, chocolate, and nuts. For a somewhat
heartier cookie, add ¼ cup whole-wheat flour, an additional
¼ cup all-purpose flour, and 2 more tablespoons bourbon.

Leah Huff 🍫 *Louisville, Kentucky*

2¼ cups flour, unsifted

1 teaspoon baking soda

½ teaspoon salt

1 cup margarine, softened

¾ cup granulated sugar

¾ cup brown sugar, firmly packed

5 tablespoons bourbon

2 eggs

9 ounces (1½ cups) milk chocolate chips

1½ cups walnuts, chopped

1. Preheat the oven to 350°F.

2. Sift together the flour, baking soda, and salt; set aside.

3. In a large mixing bowl, cream the margarine with the sugars. Beat in the bourbon and eggs. Stir in the softened ingredients, then gently stir in the chocolate chips and walnuts.

4. Drop by teaspoonfuls onto lightly greased baking sheets, spacing well apart. Bake for about 10 minutes, or until cookies are light brown. Remove from pans while still warm.

Yield: about 4 dozen

Clipper Chocolate Chipper

This is an adaptation of a cookie served on a Caribbean island cruise ship. Serve warm from the oven to bring out the hazelnut and coffee flavors of the Frangelico and Tía Maria liqueurs.

Lelia N. Hillger 🍫 St. Louis, Missouri

1 cup granulated sugar

1 cup brown sugar

2 cups butter

1½ tablespoons baking soda

¼ cup Frangelico liqueur

¼ cup Tía Maria liqueur

1 tablespoon salt

3 eggs

6 cups pastry flour

24 ounces (4 cups) semi-sweet chocolate chips

¼ cup pecans, chopped

¼ cup walnuts, chopped

1. Preheat the oven to 350°F.

2. In a large mixing bowl, cream together the sugars, butter, baking soda, liqueurs, and salt until the mixture is light and creamy. Add the eggs, beating after each addition until well blended.

3. Stir in the flour, chocolate chips, and nuts, and mix until well blended.

4. Drop by tablespoons onto greased baking sheets, spacing well apart. Flatten the cookies slightly with moistened fingers or the back of spoon. Bake for 8 to 10 minutes, or until cookies are golden brown.

Yield: about 5 dozen

Creamy Delightful Chip

Irish Mist and chocolate — the two smooth tastes are elegantly complementary. And for the ultimate antidote to a cold, damp winter's day, serve a batch of these fresh from the oven with a pot of tea enhanced by a splash of Irish Mist.

Kathy York 🍫 *Louisville, Kentucky*

2½ cups flour

1 teaspoon baking soda

½ teaspoon salt

1 cup margarine, softened

1 cup brown sugar, firmly packed

¼ cup granulated sugar

1 egg, beaten

1 package (8 ounces) cream cheese, softened

12 ounces (2 cups) semi-sweet chocolate chips, divided

¼ cup Irish Mist

1 cup pecans, chopped

1. Preheat the oven to 375°F.

2. Sift together the flour, baking soda, and salt; set aside.

3. In a large mixing bowl, cream together the margarine and sugars. Add the egg and mix well. Add the sifted ingredients to the margarine mixture.

4. In a glass bowl in the microwave or in a small pan on the stove, heat the cream cheese and one third of the chocolate chips until soft. Add the Irish Mist to the chocolate and cheese mixture. Add all of this to the first mixture. Gently stir in the rest of the chocolate chips and the nuts.

5. Drop by teaspoonfuls onto lightly greased cookie sheets. Bake for 8 to 10 minutes, or until firm.

Yield: about 6 dozen

Cable Car Chocolate Wheels

Serve as a special dessert topped with chocolate ice cream, hot fudge sauce, whipped cream, and chocolate sprinkles.

Irene E. Souza 🍫 Sunnyvale, California

3 cups flour

2 teaspoons baking soda

1½ teaspoons salt

½ cup graham cracker crumbs (about 3½ whole crackers)

1 cup margarine

½ cup unsalted (sweet) butter

1½ cups granulated sugar

1 cup light brown sugar, firmly packed

4 eggs

2 tablespoons Grand Marnier or amaretto liqueur

12 ounces (2 cups) semi-sweet chocolate chips

2 cups chopped mixed nuts

1. Preheat the oven to 350°F.

2. Combine the flour, baking soda, salt, and graham cracker crumbs; set aside.

3. In a large bowl, combine the margarine, butter, and sugars, and beat with an electric mixer at high speed until light and fluffy (about 5 minutes). Add the eggs, one at a time, beating well after each addition. Add the liqueur. Mix the dry ingredients into the creamed mixture until well blended. Stir in the chocolate chips and nuts by hand.

4. Drop by scant quarter-cupfuls onto lightly greased baking sheets, spacing cookies about 3 inches apart. Bake for 16 to 18 minutes, or until cookies are golden brown. Watch carefully; these cookies brown very quickly. Transfer to racks to cool.

Yield: about 5 dozen

Crème de Chip Cookies

You may substitue English walnuts for black walnuts, if you're not lucky enough to live where black walnut trees are abundant. These cookies pack an extra wallop with the chocolate and crème de cacao.

Patricia Neaves 🍪 Kansas City, Missouri

12 ounces (2 cups) semi-sweet chocolate chips

½ cup crème de cacao, divided

1¾ cups flour

1½ teaspoons baking powder

¼ teaspoon salt (optional)

1 cup brown sugar, firmly packed

⅓ cup vegetable oil

2 eggs, beaten

1 cup coarsely chopped black walnuts

1 cup confectioners' sugar

1. Soak the chocolate chips in the crème de cacao for about 30 minutes.

2. While the chips are soaking, sift together the flour, baking powder, and salt; set aside.

3. Drain the crème de cacao from the chips and save. Combine 1 cup of the chips, ¼ cup of the crème de cacao, the brown sugar, and the oil in a deep saucepan. Cook over medium-low heat, stirring constantly until the chips are melted. Remove from the heat.

4. Add the eggs and beat well. Beat in the sifted ingredients until thoroughly mixed. Add the nuts and the remaining chips and crème de cacao; mix well.

5. Chill the dough for about an hour, or until it can be shaped into balls with your hands.

6. Preheat the oven to 350°F.

7. Form teaspoonfuls of dough into small, loose balls. Roll the balls in confectioners' sugar and space about 2 inches apart on lightly greased baking sheets. Bake for 10 to 12 minutes. Remove from the pans to cool completely, then store in an airtight container.

Yield: 4 to 5 dozen

Coconut Chocolate Chip Cookies

Coconut, combined with Kahlúa, with its coffee and molasses flavors, makes an interesting complement to chocolate.

Kathleen A. Rosebrough   Southfield, Michigan

2¼ cups flour

1 teaspoon baking soda

⅔ cup butter, softened

¾ cup light brown sugar, firmly packed

¼ cup granulated sugar

⅓ cup Kahlúa

1 package (four-serving size) vanilla instant pudding mix

2 eggs

12 ounces (2 cups) semi-sweet chocolate chips

1 cup chopped pecans

½ cup flaked coconut

1. Mix together the flour and baking soda; set aside.

2. In a large mixing bowl, combine the butter, sugars, Kahlúa, and pudding mix, and beat until smooth and creamy. Beat in the eggs. Gradually blend in the dry ingredients, then the chocolate chips, nuts, and coconut. Chill the dough for 1 to 2 hours.

3. Preheat the oven to 375°F.

4. Form the dough into walnut-sized balls, or drop by rounded teaspoonfuls onto ungreased baking sheets, spacing about 2 inches apart. Bake at 375°F for about 9 minutes, or until golden brown.

Yield: 5 dozen

Grand Marnier
Chocolate Chip Cookies

Combining the sophisticated tastes of orange-flavored Grand Marnier and orange peel dilutes the sugary sweetness of the traditional cookie.

Ainslie Bruneau 🍫 *Lee, Massachusetts*

2½ cups flour

2 teaspoons baking powder

¼ teaspoon salt

1 cup margarine

¾ cup brown sugar, firmly packed

½ cup granulated sugar

2 eggs, well beaten

½ tablespoon Grand Marnier

1 tablespoon grated orange zest

12 ounces (2 cups) semisweet chocolate chips

1 cup chopped walnuts

Glaze:

6 ounces semisweet baking chocolate

1 tablespoon Grand Marnier

½ cup finely chopped walnuts

1. Preheat the oven to 325°F.

2. Sift the flour before measuring, then sift again with the baking powder and salt; set aside.

3. In a large mixing bowl, cream the margarine and sugars until the mixture is light and fluffy. Add the eggs and blend well. Add the sifted ingredients to the creamed mixture together with the Grand Marnier and orange zest. Mix thoroughly. Fold in the chocolate chips and nuts.

4. Drop by rounded teaspoonfuls onto ungreased baking sheets, spacing well apart. Bake for about 20 minutes. Remove from pans and cool completely.

5. For the glaze, melt the chocolate in a double boiler over hot, but not boiling, water. Remove from the heat and beat in the Grand Marnier. Coat the undersides of the cool cookies with the glaze, then dip the cookies in the chopped nuts. Refrigerate for a few minutes, until the glaze is firm. As a variation, omit the nuts and pour the glaze in stripes over the tops of the cookies.

Yield: about 4 dozen

Chocolate Chip Almond Cookies

This candylike cookie features a sugary almond coating.

Bob and Carla Witmer 🍫 *Colorado Springs, Colorado*

3½ cups flour

1 teaspoon baking soda

1 teaspoon salt

1 teaspoon cream of tartar

1 cup butter, softened

1 cup granulated sugar

1 cup light brown sugar, *not* packed

1 cup vegetable oil

1 egg

1 teaspoon vanilla extract

2 teaspoons amaretto liqueur

1 cup rolled oats

8 ounces milk chocolate, grated

12 ounces (2 cups) semi-sweet chocolate minichips

3 cups chopped almonds

6 tablespoons confectioners' sugar

2 egg whites, beaten slightly

1. Combine the flour, baking soda, salt, and cream of tartar; set aside.

2. In a large mixing bowl, cream together the butter and sugars. Blend in the oil, egg, vanilla, and amaretto. Gradually add the dry ingredients, along with the rolled oats, until the mixture is well blended. Gently stir in the grated milk chocolate and the chocolate chips. Chill until firm.

3. Preheat the oven to 375°F.

4. Mix together the chopped almonds and confectioners' sugar. Form the dough into 1-inch balls. Dip the balls into the beaten egg whites, then roll them in the almond-sugar mixture. Place on lightly greased baking sheets, spacing well apart. Bake for 8 to 10 minutes or until golden brown. Cool slightly before removing to cooling racks.

Yield: 8 to 9 dozen

Cream Cheese and Chocolate Chip Wheels

Inspired by a love for truffles, this is the cookie to bake when you have time on your hands and feel like being creative in the kitchen.

Betty Jane Robinson ⬩ Stillwater, Oklahoma

8 ounces cream cheese, very cold and firm, divided

7 tablespoons confectioners' sugar, divided

1½ cups flour

½ teaspoon baking soda

¼ teaspoons salt

½ cup butter, softened to room temperature

½ cup chunky peanut butter, at room temperature

½ cup brown sugar, firmly packed

¼ cup granulated sugar

1 teaspoon vanilla extract

1 teaspoon rum flavoring

2 jumbo eggs, beaten

¾ cup black walnuts, finely chopped

12 ounces (2 cups) semisweet chocolate chips, divided

2 tablespoons unsweetened cocoa

1. Set aside 4 ounces of the cream cheese to soften to room temperature.

2. On an 18-inch strip of waxed paper, sprinkle 4 tablespoons of the confectioners' sugar down the center in a line about 3 inches wide by 12 inches long. Cut the cold cream cheese into four 1-ounce strips. Place the pieces end to end along the line of sugar. Reaching underneath the waxed paper, roll the pieces of cheese over the sugar to coat them completely and form a long roll of sugared cheese. Continue rolling inside the waxed paper until the cheese is about ½ to ¾ inch in diameter. Place the roll of cheese in the refrigerator to keep cold and firm.

3. Mix together the flour, baking soda, and salt; set aside.

4. In a large mixing bowl, combine the butter, peanut butter, sugars, and remaining 4 ounces of softened cream cheese, and cream well.

5. Mix the vanilla and the rum flavoring with the beaten eggs, then beat into the creamed mixture until well blended. Stir in the dry ingredients. Stir in the nuts and all but ¼ cup of the chocolate chips. Refrigerate the dough at least 30 minutes.

6. Mix together the cocoa and the remaining confectioners' sugar. Drop heaping tablespoonfuls of the chilled dough into the cocoa mixture and roll to coat; be careful *not* to allow the cocoa to become mixed with the dough. Place the coated cookie balls onto ungreased baking sheets and flatten to about ½-inch thick with the bottom of a glass.

7. Slice off ¼-inch-thick pieces of the chilled cream cheese roll and press one slice flat into the center of each cookie. Allow the cookies to set for about 15 minutes.

8. Preheat the oven to 350°F.

9. Press a chocolate chip, pointed end down, into each cream cheese center so that the flat bottom of the chip extends slightly above the cheese. (Small pieces of black walnut can be substituted for chocolate chips.)

10. Bake for 12 minutes. Cool on baking sheets for about 4 minutes before removing to cooling racks.

Yield: 4 dozen

Top Hat Chocolate Chip Bars

Bar cookies save time and often seem even richer than traditional cookies. This unusual pastry is topped with chocolate-flavored cream cheese, nuts, and chocolate chips.

Hilda Garey 🍪 St. Albans, Vermont

2 cups flour

1 teaspoon baking soda

1⅔ cups granulated sugar, divided

2 eggs

¾ cup water

⅓ cup oil

1 teaspoon vanilla extract

16 ounces cream cheese, softened to room temperature

¼ cup unsweetened cocoa

½ teaspoon salt

1 cup chopped nuts

12 ounces (2 cups) semi-sweet chocolate chips

1. Preheat the oven to 350°F.

2. Mix together the flour, baking soda, and 1 cup of the sugar. Add 1 of the eggs and the water, oil, and vanilla, and stir until well blended.

3. Spread the batter on a 15- x 10-inch greased baking sheet. Bake for 15 minutes.

4. While this is baking, combine the cream cheese, the remaining sugar, the cocoa, the salt, and the remaining egg; cream well. At the end of the 15-minute baking period, spread the cheese mixture over the hot base and return the pan to the oven; continue to bake for another 15 minutes. Remove from the oven. While still hot, sprinkle the nuts and chips over the top. Cut into squares.

5. You may form cookie "sandwiches" by placing squares on top of each other, cheese sides facing, while they are still warm. Cool completely before storing in the refrigerator.

Yield: 2 to 3 dozen

INDEX

Metric Conversion Chart

Use the following chart for converting U.S. measurements to metric. Since these conversions are not exact, it's important to convert the measurements for all of the ingredients to maintain the same proportions as the original recipe.

To convert to	When measurement given is	Multiply it by
milliliters	teaspoons	4.93
milliliters	tablespoons	14.79
milliliters	fluid ounces	29.57
milliliters	cups	236.59
liters	cups	0.236
milliliters	quarts	946.36
liters	quarts	0.946
grams	ounces	28.35
kilograms	pounds	0.454
centimeters	inches	2.54

Other Storey Titles You Will Enjoy

The Apple Cookbook, by Olwen Woodier. This book features unusual recipes that use North America's favorite fruit in beverages, appetizers, snacks, brunches, entrees, and desserts. 160 pages. Paperback. ISBN 0-88266-523-5.

The Bread Book, by Ellen Foscue Johnson. There's nothing like homemade bread prepared the old-fashioned way. With foolproof instructions for the beginning baker, anyone can rise to the occasion! Offers 140 recipes from around the world, including special breads for every season and every occasion. 240 pages. Paperback. ISBN 0-88266-701-7.

Herbal Sweets, by Ruth Bass. Mint, sage, lemon balm, and many other herbs make surprisingly delicious additions to sweets of all kinds — cookies, candy, cakes, cheesecakes, punches, tarts, ice cream, and more! 64 pages. Hardcover. ISBN 0-88266-922-2.

Keeping Entertaining Simple: 500 Tips for Carefree Gatherings, by Martha Storey. This fun-to-read book offers hundreds of ideas for low-fuss, low-anxiety entertaining. 176 pages. Paperback. ISBN 1-58017-056-0.

The Maple Syrup Cookbook, by Ken Haedrich. Using maple syrup as the sugar ingredient, these recipes include the classics plus unusual relishes, delicious breads, and mouthwatering desserts. 144 pages. Paperback. ISBN 0-88266-523-5.

500 Treasured Country Recipes from Martha Storey and Friends, by Martha Storey and Friends. This heirloom cookbook presents more than 500 tried-and-true country-cooking recipes, from blueberry pancakes to chicken and dumplings to strawberry-rhubarb pie. It also covers the skills of the country kitchen, such as making cheese and sausage, preserving tomatoes, baking bread, pulling taffy, and making ice cream. 544 pages. Paperback. ISBN 1-58017-291-1.

These books and other Storey books are available at your bookstore, farm store, garden center, or directly from Storey Books, Schoolhouse Road, Pownal, Vermont 05261, or by calling 800-441-5700. Or visit our Web site at www.storeybooks.com